FAST FORWARD INVESTING

HOW TO PROFIT FROM ARTIFICIAL INTELLIGENCE, ROBOTICS, AND OTHER TECHNOLOGIES RESHAPING OUR LIVES

JON D. MARKMAN

New York Chicago San Francisco Athens London Madrid
Mexico City Milan New Delhi Singapore Sydney Toronto

1 2 3 4 5 6 7 8 9   LCR   23 22 21 20 19 18

ISBN   978-1-260-13221-2
MHID   1-260-13221-8

e-ISBN   978-1-260-13222-9
e-MHID   1-260-13222-6

This publication is designed to provide accurate and authoritative information in regard to the subject matter covered. It is sold with the understanding that neither the author nor the publisher is engaged in rendering legal, accounting, securities trading, or other professional services. If legal advice or other expert assistance is required, the services of a competent professional person should be sought.
—*From a Declaration of Principles Jointly Adopted by a Committee of the American Bar Association and a Committee of Publishers and Associations*

Library of Congress Cataloging-in-Publication Data

Names: Markman, Jon D., 1958– author.
Title: Fast forward investing : how to profit from artificial intelligence, robotics, and other technologies reshaping our lives / Jon D. Markman.
Description: New York : McGraw-Hill, [2019]
Identifiers: LCCN 2018027543| ISBN 9781260132212 (alk. paper) | ISBN 1260132218
Subjects: LCSH: Investment analysis. | Investments. | Technological innovations—Economic aspects.
Classification: LCC HG4529 .M3748 2019 | DDC 332.6—dc23 LC record available at https://lccn.loc.gov/2018027543

McGraw-Hill Education products are available at special quantity discounts to use as premiums and sales promotions or for use in corporate training programs. To contact a representative, please visit the Contact Us pages at www.mhprofessional.com.

I dedicate this book to my children, Joseph and Janie, who will see many of the exciting technologies described in this book move from the fringe to the norm, and will help shape the next generation's view of the future. I would also like to acknowledge the contributions of my excellent researcher, TB, and my wife, Ellen.

CONTENTS

INTRODUCTION

The world is accelerating at an exponentially brisk pace toward a future in which cars drive themselves, software writes itself, faulty human genetic code edits itself, and the computing power helping all of this happen is virtually limitless.

It is an era when *fast forward* is not just a button on a remote control; it is a description and an aspiration for entrepreneurs, workers, government officials, programmers, and physicians.

The stretch of time that lies ahead has the potential to create the greatest economic boom that the world has ever known, surpassing the periods that featured the discovery of fire, the discovery of electricity, the magic of flight, or the invention of computers themselves. Every impressive technology we have seen up to now has just been a prelude.

Fast forward: It is a dream and reality at the same time, as yesterday's science fiction becomes toys for children today, and crazy ideas like robotic trucks, Mach 1 ground transportation, drone armies, and highly intelligent and adaptive home furnishings are becoming a plausible reality.

All of this is going to make entrepreneurs and their backers very wealthy, but public shareholders will benefit too, and grandly. And that's the subject of this book.

This book chronicles how all of the building blocks are coming together, each augmenting the previous ones, enabling visionary entrepreneurs to build truly transformational businesses. I will show how powerful cloud networks democratized supercomputing, leading to groundbreaking changes in genomics and artificial intelligence. I will show how the rise of inexpensive sensors helped researchers turn the physical world into ethereal digital bits, and how information scientists are harnessing that data to build revolutionary software that is changing how products are built, and how services are delivered.

Also I will show the applications that are possible when all of these blocks come together. Get ready for self-driving cars, gene editing, and advances in life sciences that will bring microscopic robots, human organs generated in labs, and medical treatments tailored to our specific genomics.

Most important, along the way, I will show you how to take advantage. I'm going to show you which trends are important, and which you should ignore. I'm going to lay out the fast forward movers and shakers, the companies building integral platforms and competitive advantages that will be difficult to reproduce. In short, I am going to show you which companies are most likely to make investors rich as they hurdle to the very edges of practice and possibility.

CHAPTER 1

CLOUD COMPUTING: THE NEW ELECTRICITY

In the late 1800s, the proliferation of cheap industrial electricity changed commerce. It led to vibrant new ecosystems that fostered further innovation.

Cloud computing is serving the same role today. It is transformational.

In this chapter I will show how Amazon.com founder Jeff Bezos created this new era with a stroke of rare insight, carving a path for a new generation of entrepreneurs to follow. You will also learn how two other entrepreneurs—Mark Zuckerberg of Facebook and Reed Hastings of Netflix—would cleverly leverage cloud computing to become legends in their own right. And you will see how companies are still racing to move their business to the cloud two decades after these pioneers lit the pathway.

But first, for valuable context, I want you to take a quick detour into history to learn how an underappreciated giant of nineteenth-century business set the tone for today's innovations by disrupting industry with the development of mass-market electricity.

Henry Burden

Henry Burden, the son of a Scottish sheep farmer, landed in upstate New York in 1819 after studying engineering at the University of Edinburgh. Dead set on making his fortune in the burgeoning American industrial complex, by 1835 he had patented machines to forge the spikes used for the railroad industry. He invented another machine that made horseshoes. His company, Burden Iron Works, astounded competitors by making 60 a minute.

Ultimately, that prowess allowed Burden to supply the Union Army during the Civil War. At the time, machine-made horseshoes were sold in 100-pound kegs. Burden sold 600,000 kegs annually, generating $2 million in sales. That's $55.4 million in 2018 dollars—serious business.

Like so many industrialists of his era, such as fellow Scottish émigré Andrew Carnegie, Burden understood that ubiquitous, cost-effective power was critical to the prosperity of his business. So in 1851, he designed a massive, on-site power generation utility. The Burden Water Wheel rose 60 feet out of Wynantskill Creek in upstate New York. The enormous steel structure was the most powerful vertical waterwheel in history. It powered two large ironworks facilities that employed hundreds of men. Puddling and heating furnaces, rivet and horseshoe machines, rotary squeezers, steam engines, and boilers were powered by the great wheel.

Inspired by this invention, all across the country industrial sites began popping up alongside rivers. Access to affordable and abundant power, generated by waterwheels, was the primary consideration.

Three decades later, George Westinghouse took power generation to the next level. The gifted young New York inventor used Siemens alternators and his keen business wits in the 1880s to figure out how to distribute affordable alternating current electricity long distances through wires to industrial sites far from waterways. Over the course of the next twenty years, business went all in. As the price of electricity fell, the market share for waterwheel-based power plunged from 100 percent to just 5 percent.

Although Burden's waterwheel became obsolete, the precedent he set lived on. Inexpensive electricity transformed the world. Working solely in his own self-interest, he inadvertently brought power to the people in the same way that the cloud would bring computing to the people in our era.

Jeff Bezos

When Amazon.com founder Jeff Bezos sat down with *60 Minutes* for the first time in 1999, the online retailer was already a phenomenon. Its product line had swollen from books to CDs and DVDs. Customers and sales had grown exponentially. Yet when asked about potential growth ahead for the company, Bezos demurred. He conceded the young industry was in a category formation period, when potential was enormous and uncountable. He sandbagged the interviewer and competitors in an effort to gain a psychological advantage, but even then he saw the bigger picture. He was already building out a network of cloud-based computer systems.

Still, he could not have known then that his fledgling Seattle online store was laying the foundation for the most significant age of invention the world has ever known. He could not have known that unprecedented wealth lay ahead—not just for him but for shareholders and thousands of entrepreneurs who would career crazily forward on his copious coattails.

Like so many successful entrepreneurs, Bezos is razor-sharp, driven, and eccentric. As a young man, he parlayed his love for mathematics and bright mind into a high-paying job as a quantitative investment analyst on Wall Street. The Princeton graduate founded Amazon.com in 1994 after leaving the hedge fund D.E. Shaw. Many years later, he would admit that starting an online bookstore then was a risk best taken by someone with less to lose. Still, he had fired up his car and moved west to Seattle, determined to not live the remainder of his life wondering what might have been.

To seed the company, he rounded up 20 investors at $50,000 apiece. That $1 million bought them a 20 percent stake in a big idea. Even by angel investor standards, the valuation was steep. But Bezos, ever the numbers guy, would not relent. He sold early investors on the idea that a virtual storefront offered unprecedented leverage. According to his models, an average online store should do 27 times as much business as a comparable brick and mortar storefront. His math, or at least his sales pitch, resonated.

When the company went public in 1997, annual sales were just $15.7 million.

After the initial public offering, flush with cash, Bezos began positioning for the future. In his original 1997 letter to shareholders, he wrote about what was essential to the new enterprise. He promised to prioritize customer service and sales growth over profitability because scale was primary to achieving the business model objectives at Amazon.com. He vowed to build shareholder value by focusing relentlessly on customer satisfaction. He pledged a lasting commitment to the three guiding principles of low prices, vast selection, and fast delivery. And he promised, above all else, to prioritize long-term growth over short-term rewards.

Under the microscope of Wall Street analysts, the ability to defer gratification is often impossible, even for established companies. Amazon.com was all of a year old as a public firm. But it was clear: Bezos was building a business that could scale. It was a wise decision.

By 2003, annual sales had rocketed to $5.23 billion. Four years later, a decade after the 1997 shareholder manifesto, annual sales had risen almost tenfold to $14.84 billion.

Throughout this exciting period, Bezos stayed true to his word. The company continued to make aggressive long-term investments, often at the expense of profitability. The company leased warehouses. It hired managers and workers at a breakneck pace. However, the most significant investment was devoted to digital infrastructure. Amazon.com built massive data centers, filled with expensive servers that ran custom software.

Customers always took for granted that their personal information and order history was collected and safely stored. Beneath the surface, the combination of digital infrastructure and data analytics was doing much more. It was funnel-

5

ing reams of structured data into a large knowledge engine and making surprisingly accurate guesses about other items patrons might like to buy on the site. Who knew buyers of Ian McEwan's novel *The Comfort of Strangers* might also be pop singer Elvis Costello fans? It was running complex cyber security. And it was plugging into a network of thousands of remote servers that were storing, managing, and processing data at previously unimagined speed.

The idea of networked computers was not new. The Internet itself is a network, and in those early years of dot-com mania, it had captured investors' attention the way cryptocurrencies did two decades later. What was different about the Amazon.com experiment was scale and application. Decisive action was required to safeguard its e-commerce platform from hackers and provide computing power to make everything run smoothly. The company had to reimagine the network. It became a massive new internal utility. Amazon Web Services included large data centers, strategically located all over the world. Collectively, tens of thousands of networked servers hummed 24/7. And all of this computing power was virtualized through custom-built Internet connections.

Then in 2002, Bezos changed everything. He sent an inter-office memo to the web services teams. The directive ordered crews to begin communicating through open application programming interfaces only. There were to be no other forms of communication. No shared direct linking. No shared memory models. No back doors whatsoever. All teams were to expose their work and design interfaces as though they were visible by outside developers. In other words, software engineers were to begin coding with application programming interfaces, or APIs, as though all of their work was available to external developers. In typical Bezos fashion, the memo ended with,

"Anyone who doesn't do this will be fired. Thank you: have a nice day!"

From that point, Amazon Web Services (AWS) became a service-oriented architecture. It also became a platform.

Company evangelists started encouraging outside developers to write modular applications that could be plugged into the secure platform. The sheer size and utility of the experiment changed information technology infrastructure. Computing power, storage, and security became ubiquitous. By 2006, AWS boasted a community 150,000 strong.

Later that year, AWS began selling its spare computing power and storage to developers, researchers, governments, and enterprises on a pay-as-you-go basis. Suddenly, anyone with a big idea and a credit card had access to a virtual supercomputer. The combination was powerful. It was like electricity. It allowed smart kids in garages and college dormitories to invent new stuff that would have otherwise been pipe dreams. It helped established companies reinvent their business models. And it helped researchers and academics better understand complexities that had been mysteries. I put my own business on AWS in 2005 and never looked back.

AWS started something. It was foundational and transformative.

From Waterwheels into the Cloud

In his 2005 seminal article, "The End of Corporate Computing," published in the *MIT Sloan Management Review,* Nicolas G. Carr predicted that businesses were about to begin buying information technology in the same way they started buying electricity in the age of Burden and Westinghouse. At the time, the theory was on the fringe. Personal computers were still very much in vogue. And corporations had invested heavily in data centers, server licensing, and committed IT departments. What Carr saw, wisely, was the significant efficiency of AWS and cloud computing. He saw how the cloud, a vast decentralized network of computers and data storage, could become a general-purpose technology, allowing corporations to free up capital.

Information technology had become vital to business. It had also become bloated and inefficient. In the race to build applications, corporations began replicating digital infrastructure. And the cost of expensive data centers, filled with thousands of servers running licensed software, was only eclipsed by the expense of paying IT administrators to check servers and software physically. Very often, labor costs exceeded the combined costs of hardware and software.

In a cloud-computing environment, infrastructure costs were borne by the provider. The virtual connection reduced administrative costs, too.

In 2005, Carr was well ahead of his time. But he was on to something. While their efforts at first seemed implausible, both Burden and Bezos were resourceful. When faced with a problem, they sharpened their pencils and made do with what they had. When they outgrew that, they invented what they needed. In the case of Burden, it was a giant waterwheel to power his ironworks plants. For Bezos, the solution was digital. He required infrastructure to store data and nourish the growing hunger for faster computing. To his credit, very early on, Bezos realized that the web services private utility he was building could ultimately serve as a general-purpose technology to other digital entrepreneurs.

As a businessman in the mid-1800s, Burden wanted all of the advantages for himself. Years later, Westinghouse erased Burden's advantages. His AC power plants changed the industrial landscape by making electric power a general-purpose technology. And just as entrepreneurs and corporations build applications atop AWS today, 130 years ago smart entrepreneurs were building applications atop electrical power infrastructure.

The stretch of time between the 1870s and the 1910s—now known as the Gilded Age—gave us much of what we consider to be the foundation of modernity: railroads, telephones, the automobile, the airplane, elevators, antibiotics, the efficient factory, radio, movies, and mass marketing.

These things might have started as the adornments of the wealthy, but by the 1890s, factory floors, hotels, amusement parks, and other public places twinkled with the incandescence of electric lights. By 1930, 70 percent of American households were wired. The Wright brothers made aviation history in 1903 when they flew an aircraft made from spare bicycle parts for 12 minutes at Kitty Hawk. Only six years later, their company provided an airplane to the US Army capable of flying for an hour before refueling.

Advances came quickly. The buzz in the air during this era was electric.

By comparison, the accomplishments of today's inventors might seem small and self-serving. That thinking is short-sighted. Information technology is even more powerful than electricity. Harnessing the cloud is allowing a new collection of bright minds to reimagine what is possible on a global scale. It is also creating wealth that dwarfs the Gilded Age.

Mark Zuckerberg

On February 4, 2004, Mark Zuckerberg and four Harvard college roommates launched Facebook. A genius introvert, Zuckerberg was curious about how some people seemed to easily form social connections. Facebook began as a simple website to connect Harvard students. As it grew, the site accepted other Ivy League schools, then Stanford, then other colleges. High school students were allowed later. Since 2006, anyone above the age of 13 has been able to create an account. Growth exploded. In 2018, Facebook had two billion account holders worldwide.

For most of the connected world, Facebook has become connective tissue. It is where people congregate, communicate, and share the news of their lives.

It is also the quintessential cloud-based business. It's thin and light and all of the heavy lifting happens in the cloud. Mumbaikars munching aloo parathas and sifting through their newsfeeds at Internet cafes get the same low latency experience as San Francisco night-clubbers posting pictures from their iPhones to Instagram.

The modularity and flexibility of cloud computing made it easy to build an ecosystem with inherent network effects.

Initially, the intuitive software helped people easily connect with their friends and family online. When the novelty of reading friends' opinions on low-carb diets wore off, Facebook moved on to photo sharing. Weddings and graduation ceremonies were big hits. Plus, it required almost no investment from members. Hit the Like button or type up a good wish and you were good to go. Genius. When photos waned, Facebook added news sharing. It thrived. The experience is addictive.

It helped that Facebook gave everything away for free, and

had the flexibility to make periodic changes on the fly to tweak the experience.

Once members were connected with the people they cared most about and hooked on the service Facebook provided, monetization was easy. All of the demographic data members volunteered in the site's terms of service is gold to advertisers. They can't find it anywhere else so cheaply.

The model is unstoppable and easily transferred to other innovative verticals. Seventy million businesses now use Facebook Business Pages. That's from a standing start in 2012. It's all vintage Facebook. It lured businesses with intuitive software and attractive terms, then found a way to make money.

For example, Facebook is encouraging businesses to bring a portion of their enterprise inside the network. Artificially intelligent bots can provide cost-effective customer services like selling tickets, buying food, and sending money. For its trouble, Facebook earns a fee only when it engages one of the businesses' customers. It is a true software-as-a-service application, built on top of Facebook, made possible by the general-purpose technology of the cloud. The business leverage that this model affords is extreme. Businesses get to free up capital now mired in call centers and customer service. And, they get to engage their customers where they are most comfortable: on Facebook.

This new business augments what the social network is already doing. So far, the financial numbers are mindboggling. In 2016, Facebook logged sales of $27.64 billion, up 54.2 percent over 2015. Mobile makes up the lion's share of that juggernaut, and it's rising steadily as Facebook clients move from PCs to their smartphone. Ironically, it wasn't long ago pundits worried the company would flounder as users made that move.

Through January 2018, the company's stand-alone mobile

applications—WhatsApp, Messenger, and Instagram—were attracting 1.2 billion, 1.2 billion, and 700 million monthly users, respectively.

And the best part, by far, is that this is only the beginning. Facebook has just started to exploit its assets. Messenger and WhatsApp are free from monetization despite their rich trove of demographic data. Meanwhile, according to eMarketer, an online engagement research firm, Instagram is expected to generate $3.92 billion in sales in 2017, mostly from advertisements and paid sponsorships.

Zuckerberg started this culture-defining business with little more than a curiosity about how people make connections and some venture capital to buy cloud computing and data storage. He didn't have to pay for expensive servers or loads of bandwidth that he might never use. And the scalability of a cloud-based business model gave him flexibility to experiment. So he played with new user interfaces. He changed the newsfeed to understand what people were sharing and why. It all helped him see and understand what elements connected people.

After all of these years, Facebook is still a work in progress. Although it is the largest social media platform in the world, Zuckerberg is still trying to understand how people make connections. In the process, he built a powerful private ecosystem on the public cloud.

Reed Hastings

In 2006, Netflix, a mail-order DVD rental company, began to transform into a digital business. It was a complete rethinking of the business model that was gobbling up market share at the expense of Blockbuster, the nationwide leader. It was also an immense technical challenge that would have been impossible without the cost efficiencies and scale on demand of cloud computing.

The idea was big, bold, and risky. For Reed Hastings, cofounder of Netflix, it all made sense. Hastings is obsessed with moving forward.

He and partner Marc Randolph thought the company could stream media content over the Internet, thereby disrupting its successful DVD rental business. At scale, it was also an untested subscription model. To make it work, Netflix engineers had to develop algorithms to compress data, ease possible bottlenecks, and find ways to store exponentially more data. They needed a digital infrastructure that could quickly scale and shrink, depending on demand. They needed to be able to add proprietary data analytics modules. And they needed everything to be safe and secure in their virtual sandbox.

It was a business model built on the public cloud. In 2006, only Amazon Web Services had the scale and architecture to make their dream a reality.

It was the second time in ten years that the tiny Scotts Valley, California, company came up with an innovative delivery concept. When it opened its doors in 1997, sending DVDs by mail seemed crazy. However, the idea was a big hit with time-deprived young families weary of paying late fees at Blockbuster. It also created an immediate problem: Netflix didn't have enough inventory of new releases. So company engineers worked with what they had. They developed an algorithm using data analytics and predictive modeling that deemphasized popular titles. Members got a personalized queue that gave them suggestions based on their interests. By 2006, new releases represented less than 30 percent of its rentals. Jonathan Cohen, the principal brand analyst at Amobee, a global technology marketing firm, points out that Netflix's success stems mostly from "using analytics to understand audiences" better than less savvy competitors.

As the company made the transition from mail-order rentals to digital streaming media, it leveraged those advantages.

When customers are curled up on the sofa, scanning their queue, ecosystems are probably the furthest thing from their mind. However, Netflix knows what summaries they're reading, how long they spend surfing titles, what they ultimately watch, and for how long. It's using all of that network data to keep them engaged and enhance their experience.

It's also using the data to develop, license, and market new content. Ted Sarandos, chief content officer, knows network data is invaluable because it allows Netflix to build a business model around narrow casting, a personalized experience for each of its subscribers. Unlike ad-dependent networks, it doesn't need blockbusters. That creates a lot of leeway.

Even when it spent $100 million for 26 episodes of "House of Cards," Netflix stacked the deck in its favor. Fans of the original British show were potential viewers of the political drama. Fans of director David Fincher and actor Kevin Spacey might also like the show, too. Netflix understood what its viewers wanted before they knew. It's an unconventional calculus that Sarandos used to build a wildly successful streaming content portfolio.

And then there are network effects. Like Facebook, Netflix is now benefitting from the impact of building a substantial business. Subscribers are enticed because their friends at work, school, or in social settings might be talking about Netflix original programming or the ease of use. The growth of its network made it more valuable to subscribers, leading to more subscribers.

In late 2017, Netflix crossed 100 million subscribers. That was roughly a threefold increase since the original "House of Cards" content deal in 2013. During that time, sales have increased from $4.37 billion to $8.83 billion.

As a result, Netflix has become a powerhouse in the motion picture business. It spent $6 billion on content in 2017. That is second only to ESPN, the Disney-owned sports broadcaster. More telling, it has become an essential part of the secondary market for episodic content. This media is critical for Netflix because it can be binge-streamed, keeping users engaged. Off-beat shows like "Mad Men" and "Breaking Bad" gained cult followings on Netflix even though they were produced and had first runs on AMC. That success allowed AMC to do more edgy shows like "The Walking Dead."

Even then, Netflix managers were always looking over their shoulders. In 2016, Hastings told the *New York Times* that the massive Netflix audience was also fostering competitors. He worried that smaller content providers were building catalogs with the critical mass to start competing services. "We knew there was no long-term business in being a rerun company, just as we knew there was no long-term business in being a DVD-rental company," he said.

Netflix's algorithmic recommendations and the personalized queue are now widely copied. In 2017, it's the standard procedure for doing digital media distribution. What sets the company apart from potential rivals is data analytics. Netflix has an intimate relationship with its members because it knows everything about viewing habits, likes, and dislikes. It uses that data to keep its customers engaged in profound new ways.

According to comScore, consumers spent 24 percent more time on Netflix during the last quarter of 2016 than they did during the same period a year prior. And, for all the fuss about its rising content costs, Netflix spends about seven cents per hour viewed on content, with Morgan Stanley estimating that traditional broadcast networks average about 13 cents per hour of content viewed.

Modularity is the key. Even with its gaudy 100 million-plus subscribers, Netflix still has no substantial investment in data centers or servers. The power of the business is software. It is data analytics. It is predictive modeling. It is original programming tailored to its target audience. The company knows its customers. It understands what they want and how to deliver.

The flexibility of the cloud allows Netflix to bolt on software to run the business. It also allows the company to scale storage and bandwidth as needed, on demand. This elasticity is only possible with the public cloud.

Hastings saw the potential to deliver content over the Internet, across multiple hardware platforms. It was a giant step forward and helped the company build a massive ecosystem with innovation at its core. Today, Netflix is the only worldwide broadcast network. It's a big business but its cloud-based infrastructure allows managers to be as nimble and innovative as a start-up.

Like Facebook, Netflix is an application with global scale, sitting on top of a powerful cloud platform. Developers use the supercomputing capabilities of the cloud to deliver up-to-date, personalized content to more than 100 million subscribers, in real time.

They also use all of the information they learn from customer behavior to develop new programming and new sources of revenue. The company is always moving forward, just like Hastings, its cofounder.

The Cloud-Computing Paradigm Shift

Today software runs car engines and GPS systems. It helps logistics companies track packages with pinpoint accuracy. Energy firms use it to find oil miles beneath the ocean floor. The US military uses it to destroy enemy targets thousands of miles away, with drone strikes.

All of it is possible because of the advances in cloud computing. It is a paradigm shift. For most of us, it means never running out of space again on our smartphone. It means there is no need to sacrifice pictures of the family vacation for Sarah's dance recital. That's just scratching the surface.

Cloud computing is not just about data storage. It's about instantaneous data analytics and scalable, powerful computing the likes of which the world has never seen. It makes possible things that were science fiction even in 2011: self-driving cars, smart cities, gene editing, real-time biometrics like facial and voice recognition, augmented reality. and on-the-fly language translation. Cloud computing brings the power of a supercomputer to any device. That's the shift. There is no need for our tools to get exponentially more robust.

Amazon Web Services, as a business, was created out of thin air when Bezos decided its web services would use open APIs. Selling its excess storage and compute power made it a utility in the same way that Burden and Westinghouse flipped a switch and changed the industrial landscape with electricity. The difference was that AWS democratized supercomputers and information technology. It allowed entrepreneurs to reimagine what was possible, and in the process, create unprecedented wealth.

Over the years, Fortune 100 companies like Facebook and Netflix were attracted. They could buy storage and compute power as needed and at a fraction of the cost of building their facilities. Businesswise, it was a no-brainer. It was cost effective, and there were no infrastructure hardware headaches.

A 2016 report from consulting firm McKinsey & Co, "IT: From Build to Consume," found that "more large enterprises are likely to move workloads away from traditional and virtualized environments toward the cloud—at a rate and pace that is expected to be far quicker than in the past."

While smaller companies and start-ups, often cash-strapped, get the same resources and cost savings, the main attraction is scale. Many have been able to develop disruptive technologies that would have been otherwise cost prohibitive.

Ride-hailing company Uber built real-time, logistics software to monitor and match up millions of riders and taxis on a global scale. Spotify made a database capable of streaming on demand any song from any album for tens of millions of customers.

All of that cheap computer power has been a boon for big research ideas, too.

GlaxoSmithKline and Alphabet's Verily are using machine learning to build tiny, implantable robots capable of zapping nerves. The bots could wipe out chronic illnesses like arthritis, Crohn's disease, and diabetes. Microsoft is writing software to store digital data on synthetic DNA. Its engineers have already been able to cram 200 MB of data onto a surface no more significant than the tip of a sharpened pencil. The entire public content of the Internet could fit into a shoebox.

Shifts this big create massive opportunities for investors.

Research firm Gartner projects the public cloud-computing sector is expected to grow to $302 billion in 2021, a near two-fold increase from $153 billion in 2017. And the future looks even brighter.

The Cloud Pioneer: Amazon.com

Facebook and Netflix are transformative applications that were enabled by the computer power, and flexibility of the cloud. However, the very first cloud business to operate at scale was **Amazon.com** (AMZN).

The massive ecommerce operation was built atop Amazon Web Services. More than a decade later, AWS is by far the leading cloud-computing business in the world.

Since 2006, when AWS hit the mainstream business world, a handful of big technology companies—Amazon, Facebook, Netflix, Salesforce.com, and Adobe—have built impressive cloud-based businesses. They transformed industries with dynamic new business models. They built best-in-class products that were scalable and available on any device with an Internet connection.

Customers voted. The innovators won.

Investors should pay attention. The cloud is the future of computing. And that inevitability will lead to breathtaking growth for companies with competitive advantages. The AWS advantage is scale, security, and developer outreach, thanks to its early adoption of APIs. Today, AWS has the biggest third-party network of any cloud vendor.

Managers also built a robust reseller program around open standards. And the AWS GovCloud, a separate secure server infrastructure launched in 2011, has made significant—and lasting—inroads into many state and federal government agencies.

In July 2014, the *Atlantic* reported a secret deal struck during 2013 between AWS and the Central Intelligence Agency. The groundbreaking $600 million, 10-year agreement stretched into all 17 intelligence agencies.

Its big selling point was that the CIA would pay only for the AWS services it used.

This pay-as-you-go model had revolutionized private IT infrastructure by radically reducing costs. In 2013, AWS brought it to the US government. As its capabilities progressed, AWS and its partner network snagged more contracts. They became more integral to future plans.

In July 2016, the State Department awarded AWS and its partner, C3 IoT, a software developer, a wide-ranging contract to provide predictive analytics and real-time access to telemetry, enterprise, and extraprise data across 22,000 facilities.

The Pentagon is expected to award AWS a 10-year contract to help the Department of Defense (DOD) operate securely in the cloud. The Joint Enterprise Defense (JED) Infrastructure program could be worth $10 billion.

According to *Business Insider*, government officials were so confident that AWS would win JED that they began making the transition to GovCloud before the deal was completed.

Considering that the DOD wants to award the contract to one company—and that it already has AWS infrastructure plus a network of approved resellers in place—the point was well taken. No other company can provide the requisite scale and security.

And the AWS franchise is just one part of Amazon.com. The original pillar of its business, e-commerce, is rock solid, and it's getting stronger every quarter as sales explode.

In August 2017, Amazon.com announced it was buying Whole Foods, an upscale grocery chain with 460 stores. It was a $14 billion deal to effectively enter food retailing, a business known for razor-thin margins. Both Whole Foods and Amazon.com shares advanced on the news.

That's not because of synergies. It's not because Amazon will increase margins. It's far simpler.

Whole Foods makes Amazon's best product way more attractive. That product is Amazon Prime. Amazon has never played by traditional big company rules. It refuses to grow up. It does not really worry about reported profits. It reinvests cash flow like a start-up. Its focus from day one through today has been securing loyal, repeat customers.

These are Prime members. They love shopping at the online retailer so much that they are willing to pay $99 per year for the privilege. It's already a $6.4 billion subscription business, and the company hinted, during a first-quarter 2018 conference call, that a $20 price increase is likely within the year.

In 2016, an analyst at Cowen and Co. calculated that Prime members spend a staggering $193 per month. And 91 percent renew after the first year. In February, he estimated the number of Prime memberships had swollen to 80 million worldwide.

Amazon built a business for which its best customers pay to join, spend a lot, and don't leave. Sweet.

It does lavish Prime members with perks. They get free music- and video-streaming services from the cloud. Free two-day shipping on parcels is standard. Among other things, they can store photos on the cloud, borrow digital reading material, and, in some zip codes, have takeout delivered for free too.

The win for Amazon is not that it will boost margins at Whole Foods. In fact, *Bloomberg* reported it will reduce prices. The win is Whole Foods makes Prime stickier, that it ramps up customer spending.

Long term, I suspect Amazon shares will reach well above $2,300, driven by its bright fundamentals and the dynamism of its flexible, cloud-based business model. The prospects for sales growth in the cloud are also solid. And with long-term customers like the CIA and, perhaps, the DOD, there's little that can keep this good company down. Its valuation may become excessive from time to time, meriting pullbacks and consolidation, but over time Amazon.com should be owned by investors who wish to put their portfolios on fast forward.

Fast Forward

In this chapter, I laid out the building blocks for this era of exponential growth. It started when Jeff Bezos did for computing power what Henry Burden did for electricity. He made it inexpensive and ubiquitous, allowing an entire generation of entrepreneurs to build transformational products and services. Mark Zuckerberg and Reed Hastings built media behemoths that changed the way we communicate and spend time. Others are following their lead by building great businesses that scale and are available to any device with an Internet connection. That is the power of cloud-based businesses. It's a huge trend that is sweeping commercial enterprises, governments, and nonprofit foundations all over the world.

The world is accelerating toward this future. The byword is fast forward, all the time, every time. Now let's dig deeper.

HOW TO PLAY: The very best way to play this transition to cloud computing is still demonstrated by Amazon.com, the company Jeff Bezos built in his Seattle garage more than two decades ago.

CHAPTER 2

SENSORS: ANALOG BECOMES DIGITAL

There are now two billion smartphones on the planet. Most of us carry one. We take their convenience and features for granted, missing the bigger picture. The mass production of smartphones has driven down the price of miniature optical, voice, and other measurement sensors. It means that it is now cost effective to record the analog world in digital snippets.

In this chapter, I will examine real-world applications for sensors and show you how the collection of digital data is leading to practical problem solving and dynamic new business models. Along the way I will call out the innovative companies leveraging new sensor technology to propel their business to new heights.

The Kodak Experience

In 1975, Steve Sasson, an engineer at Eastman Kodak, invented the first digital camera sensor. It was the size of a toaster. Its data was recorded on cassette tape. The only way to view the grainy, black-and-white image was on a TV.

He took the prototype to the Kodak board of directors. Young and ambitious, he expected they would see the sensor's huge potential. His eight-pound device circumvented many of the weaknesses of current cameras. It was not limited by the size of camera rolls. It was not prone to mechanical failure because there were no moving parts. Yet what the directors saw was a bulky contraption that didn't use Eastman Kodak chemicals or paper. They killed the idea.

Twenty years later, that turndown killed Kodak's photography business.

In fairness, neither Sasson nor Kodak executives could have known digital sensor development would proceed so quickly. At the time the idea, although novel, seemed entirely impractical. There was no market for a cumbersome camera that required a screen to view its pictures. Moving forward would have been reckless and potentially disruptive to Kodak's core business.

Today, the progeny of that sensor can be found inside every smartphone. These sensors are dramatically improved in every way. They are smaller, cheaper, more accurate, and less fussy. They see and record more. And years of constant refinement have made them modular. Digital camera sensors have become utilitarian.

Devices like these are the sensory organs of the new digital age. They help our machines see; they are the intake valves of new information; they are a network of hidden observers and spies—constantly gathering data through microphones, counters, and gyros for further processing in the cloud. They are the largely hidden heroes that are accelerating our era into fast-forward mode. And the companies that develop, make, distribute, manipulate, analyze, and service them are some of the most successful of the past five years, and will become even more valuable in the next five years.

Hardware developers are using these tools and their spinoffs to digitize, capture, replicate, and reshape the physical world. Like Sasson four decades ago, they are turning real-world events into software and data. That information has incredible value—and in the right hands it will be exploited at warp speed to enhance lives, productivity, corporate balance sheets, and the greater good.

Let's check out some examples of both private and public companies, and I'll explore three important companies that bear consideration by serious investors.

Tiny Satellites Are a Big Opportunity

A private company called Planet Labs has set a remarkable goal: Survey our entire planet continuously from space. Its tiny, low-orbit satellites are constantly at work snapping high-resolution photos of Iowa cornfields, Russian oil pads, and much more.

The company was founded in 2010 as Cosmogia. A trio of NASA engineers became intrigued by the development of smartphones. Even then, the devices had more processing power and better sensors than very expensive satellites. They saw a rare opportunity to disrupt aerospace.

It was a strange time. In the wake of the financial crisis,

budgets were under pressure. NASA was desperately trying to encourage smaller companies and research organizations to get involved. Its Solar Dynamics Observatory had launched in February at a staggering cost of $850 million. And the price tag for Genesis—its low-cost, sun particle–collecting satellite—swelled to $164 million. Something had to give.

The solution was Fast Affordable Science Technology Satellites (FASTSATs).

The big idea was to use the sensors common in modern smartphones to build a new breed of low-orbit, cost-effective satellites. NASA engineers Chris Boshuizen and Will Marshall were dispatched to make it happen. Ultimately, a team they started launched three minisatellites in 2013: Alexander, Graham, and Bell. Named after the telephone inventor, the pint-sized satellites got into space and beamed back high-resolution pictures for just $7,000.

By that time, Boshuizen, Marshall, and Robbie Schingler were hard at work running Planet Labs. They wanted to make even smaller, less expensive satellites using a software model. They built a prototype. Then they determined how to make it work with software modeling, off-the-shelf sensors, and cheap smartphone components. Their ambition and early success attracted venture capitalists.

In 2014, Planet Labs dropped a flock of 28 miniature satellites, called Doves, into low orbit from the International Space Station. Iteration continued. Like smartphones, every new model got better specification and became less expensive. The company now has 130 low-orbiting Doves in operation. It is enough to produce high-resolution imagery of the entire planet every 24 hours.

The company is effectively indexing Earth every hour as its cameras snap 1.5 million pictures per day. Even with government satellites, this has never been possible. And it will only improve and speed up as the company uses algorithms and machine learning to make greater sense of its trove of empirical data.

The business applications are immediately obvious. Such precise, up-to-the-minute data allows insurance companies to verify claims. It allows oil drillers to monitor site safety. Investment analysts can glean insights about crop yields, container shipments, or even shopping mall traffic.

All of this data can be aggregated with other empirical data sets to derive even greater insights. The potential uses are unlimited. The importance of the data is unmatched.

And it is all the result of the exponential improvement of sensors, coupled with declining costs.

Reimagining Metal Mining

Mining giant **Rio Tinto PLC** (RIO) is willing to go to hell and back for copper.

Its new mine near Superior, Arizona, bores nearly 7,000 feet below the Earth's surface. There, temperatures routinely hit 175 degrees Fahrenheit. Warm water falls from overhead rocks like rain. The 1.3-mile-deep shaft is being excavated by Resolution Copper Mining, a subsidiary of London-based Rio Tinto and Australia-based **BHP Billiton Ltd.** (BHP). It's a project no sane executive would have green-lighted a decade ago. The technical challenges are that daunting. The attraction is the opportunity to change the business of mining. Sensors, autonomous vehicles, and data analytics make that possible.

It wouldn't be the first time technology changed the landscape of the natural resources industry. Just as data analytics and advanced modeling made it easier to fracture shale and find natural gas, these tools will figure prominently in the mining activity of Resolution.

After engineers figure out how to deal with the heat and the water, they plan to completely reimagine mining. **Caterpillar Inc. (CAT)** and Komatsu Mining Corp. are already building custom electric loaders, excavators, and other robotic gear. They will be equipped with thousands of sensors to achieve 360-degree data acquisition and analytics that can result in full automation.

The machines will find the ore, mine it, and transport it to the surface under the watchful eye of technicians hundreds of miles away.

None of this has come cheap. The *Wall Street Journal* reports that the project will cost at least $6 billion. And operation is not scheduled to begin until the mid-2020s, thanks to the regulatory process.

However, the payoff is potentially huge. The mining industry has exhausted the supply of easy-to-find, high-grade copper ore available at open pit mines. Copper deposits exist, but they are hard to reach. The Resolution mine may have 1.6 billion tons of ore and a 40-year productive life.

Obtaining those deposits is more important than ever. Copper plays an outsized role in electric vehicles, or EVs, which now represent a fraction of vehicles sold—but their numbers are growing quickly.

BHP, a minority partner in the Resolution project, expects there will be 140 million EVs on the road by 2035. In early 2018 there were around one million. The *Financial Times* reports that EVs use roughly four times as much copper as internal combustion cars.

If BHP is right, and EVs displace 8 percent of traditional

vehicles by 2035, the math works out to 8.5 million tons of new demand. That is about one-third of the total current demand. You can imagine what that imbalance would do to copper prices.

More importantly, think about the new business models possible. Think about the opportunities available to astute investors willing to look into the future.

Increased computing power, robotics, and sensors allowed Rio Tinto executives to dream about mining copper more than a mile below the Earth's surface—and execute on it.

In the Blink of an Eye

How cool would it be to take snapshots or record video simply by blinking your eye? It would be a superpower, and it's also coming sooner than you think.

Alphabet, Sony, and Samsung have all filed patents for contact lens systems that use tiny electronic antennas and optical sensors to record video and take pictures. The technology is real. It is happening.

A contact lens with a built-in camera certainly pushes the limit of what most people believe is possible. It is not hard to imagine augmented reality and other cool applications. Police officers would be able to identify suspects by surveying a crowd. Paramedics might gain access to a victim's medical records after visual identification. Add an earpiece and a network connection, and first responders would suddenly have superpowers.

The concept was science fiction until 2009. That's when researchers at the University of Washington managed to successfully test a prototype that involved an integrated circuit, a radio receiver, and a light emitting diode (LED).

In 2016, DARPA, the research division for the Department of Defense, challenged the technology community to dramatically reduce the size of printed circuit boards through modularity. The goal is to shrink the time and energy required to move data by making PCBs much smaller.

DARPA has its own motives.

Officials claim the new architecture would be perfect for applications like identifying objects in real-time video feeds, and coordinating fast-moving swarms of unmanned aerial vehicles.

It would also help shrink the electronics required for a contact lens camera system.

So far, all of the patents filed by major technology companies involve a multilayered system. There is an antenna to wirelessly transfer data to another device, like a smartphone. There is a circuitry component, involving a microprocessor and autofocus image pickup sensor. The Sony patent makes reference to onboard storage, but it's not clear how that would work.

For power, each patent experiments with some form of kinetic energy. The idea is to harness the power created from natural blinking. Somehow, the devices will differentiate deliberate blinking, which will control the user interface. It all seems incredibly complicated.

Then again, we are talking about a tiny sensor attached to a contact lens.

Farming on the Steppes of San Francisco

Plenty, a San Francisco agricultural technology company, has a great name. It also has a compelling vertical farming idea that could change agriculture forever. And it is all because the cost of sensors is plummeting.

In 2017, Plenty scored $200 million in financing from Softbank, the Japanese firm led by billionaire Masayoshi Son, and investment companies associated with Alphabet chairman Eric Schmidt and Amazon founder Jeff Bezos.

These well-heeled investors are betting on big disruption. Investors should pay attention.

Farming has not changed much in centuries. Sure, there are self-driving tractors and even drones, but the basic process still involves sowing seeds and waiting patiently for Mother Nature to bless the soil with bountiful crops.

Plenty wants to change all of that.

As you might expect, given its Bay area roots, the company is looking to supercharge farming with information technology and a healthy dose of idealism.

According to a story at the website Inhabitat, Plenty claims advances in data science and microsensors will limit the use of water by 99 percent. For some crops, LED lighting, humidity control, and planting techniques can push yields to 350 times more than of a typical farm. And all produce will be free of pesticides, herbicides, and GMOs.

And because the farms are indoors and no bigger than a suburban Walmart or Home Depot, they can be placed near large urban populations.

That's where the idealism kicks in.

Plenty made getting nutritious, organic food close to the people part of its mission statement. A company blog explains that over the past several decades, foods have actually become less rich in vitamins and minerals. As weird as that seems, agriculture as a business changed from a patchwork of local farms to large international agribusinesses.

Innovation is focused on the economics of 3,000-mile supply chains. Fruits and vegetables are engineered to withstand the scars of long truck rides and the bruises of extended stays on shipping docks.

Matt Barnard, Plenty's young chief executive, has a different take on innovation. Controlling every aspect of the environment reduces costs. Reducing the farm footprint puts produce closer to the market. It also means the company can experiment with heirloom seeds like Black Vernissage tomatoes and Violetta Italia cauliflower.

Shrinking the supply chain to 50 miles has its tasty advantages.

In many ways, vertical farming is the type of innovation science fiction promised years ago. It just makes sense. However, even five years ago the economics did not make sense. Falling prices for cloud computing, machine learning, and sensors have been the key.

Information technology is being commoditized by sensors—just like fruits, vegetables, and livestock.

That commoditization is changing entire sectors. It is quickly reinvigorating old business models and inventing new ones like vertical farming.

It's the type of change most investors miss—only at their peril.

The New Gilded Age

Admittedly, investing in any market in which the underlying asset has become a commodity carries outsized risk. For centuries, speculators have prospered and gone broke in the tumult of cotton, grain, livestock, and energy prices. Those markets are subject to unknowable variables like weather.

Something different is happening with information technology.

I have often compared the current era to the Gilded Age. In the decades following the end of the Civil War through the early 1900s, American industry changed. It was not only the advent of industrialization. It was something bigger. Companies—guided by tycoons such as Andrew Carnegie, J.P. Morgan, and John D. Rockefeller—began to grow dramatically larger. They integrated both vertically and horizontally. They either consumed their competitors through merger, or they simply reduced prices to levels that made production unprofitable at smaller outfits.

This was possible because they had better access to information. And they had scale. These competitive advantages ensured their longer-term profitability.

If you survey the current IT landscape, these themes become readily apparent. Industry leaders have substantial intellectual property portfolios, and they have overwhelming scale. In most mature markets, there is no reason for competitors to enter because they cannot possibly manufacture at competitive rates. And when they can, due to innovation, they are quickly bought out by an industry leader.

For example, Sony and Samsung dominate digital camera sensors. Developers looking for optical sensors begin in

Japan and Korea because there they will get the best prices and equipment.

Eastman Kodak filed for bankruptcy protection in 2012. The upstate New York company, founded in 1888, sold its vast intellectual property portfolio for a paltry $525 million. The buyers were a consortium of Apple, Google, Amazon.com, Microsoft, Samsung, Adobe Systems, and the Taiwanese firm HTC.

The opportunity for investors is niche markets. Due to the nature of sensors, there are smaller companies that have built massive IP portfolios and economies of scale. As the market for their products grows exponentially in the digital era, they stand to become much bigger businesses.

Helping Robots to See: The Case for Cognex Corp.

Cognex Corp. (CGNX) is the leading maker of sensors and vision systems for industrial robots. Its technology is a prerequisite for Industry 4.0 and the rise of smart factories.

For a long time, smart factories were a pipe dream. Robots were impressive for their might. But they were dumb. They didn't have eyes. They could not make sense of their place in the process. They stamped or welded or pushed items along a precision conveyor belt.

All of that changed with Cognex Insight Vision systems. They are the heart and soul of the modern industrial manufacturing complex.

The company was founded in 1981 by Robert Shillman, a lecturer at MIT, and two graduate students. Its DataMan vision system, released in 1982, read, verified, and assured the quality of letters and numbers using optical character recognition. Since that time, there has been a flurry of acquisitions to build its IP portfolio.

In the automotive world (home to most of the expensive industrial robots), vision sensors, camera systems, and custom software from the Massachusetts company are now the industry standard. They can be bolted onto a wide variety of robots with ease. Their scanners survey the production of automobile brake pads. Their 3D systems detect imperfections invisible to the human eye. The result is drastically improved product quality, less down time, and a better return on investment.

The company's systems also play a role in every step of the production of modern internal combustion engines. Vision tools identify serial numbers with OCR algorithms. Robots, fitted with 2D vision systems, inspect, pick, and position metal for fabrication. And 3D vision scanners ensure quality by passing over welds, rivets, and adhesive applications.

For financial officers, the investment is a no-brainer. The process pays for itself.

In airports, its baggage system is capable of scanning 900 bags per hour. It can spot defective tags and separate suspicious items. As the world builds new airports at a heady clip, and security becomes more pressing, Cognex's systems are in high demand.

The company is already growing fast. In October 2017, the company reported a 76 percent increase in third-quarter sales, to $259.74 million. That eclipsed the consensus view by $3.36 million. Income during the quarter rose to $102.35 million, a 91 percent increase over a year ago.

Although Cognex has been in business for 36 years, its business is now accelerating. During the last five years, sales growth has been explosive. The compound annual rate of growth is 24 percent.

Cognex logged $521 million in sales in 2016. Through the first nine months of 2017, sales surged to $567 million. This is certain to increase as companies spend to make factories more efficient, and governments invest in airport security.

Cloud computing, big data, and cognitive computing are coming to robotics. The payoff is simply too big to ignore. To get there, managers need to invest in vision systems. Cognex builds best-in-class systems. Its platform is being run by every leading auto company. It is a likely winner.

HOW TO PLAY: Cognex shares were up 690 percent during the past five years through early 2018. This growth story is far from over. The shares are still buyable for new investors.

Heat Seeking Vision: Flir Systems

Flir Systems (FLIR) is the world's largest maker of thermal imaging cameras, components, and imaging sensors.

Through the years, the Oregon company has been a slow and steady grower. Its sensors were consumed by the military and the recreational vehicle market. That era is coming to an end. The company is now actively pursuing automotive markets. In the age of advanced driver-assistance systems and self-driving cars, that is a big opportunity for investors.

Most laypeople would be hard-pressed to point to a Flir product. The company builds highly technical gear used for surveillance, scientific instrumentation, maritime, and security and detection applications.

Its Ranger HRC is a network-enabled, long-range camera system. It can spot enemy troops ten kilometers away. Star Safire is a state-of-the-art intelligence, surveillance, reconnaissance, and targeting system used on attack helicopters. And its PD-Black Hornet provides those same capabilities to troops in the field. It looks like a tiny toy helicopter, but it's the world's smallest drone. And it's packed with Flir imaging technology.

Its gear is also well regarded by first responders, border security agents, tradespeople, scientists, and recreational vehicle enthusiasts. A good thermal setup can help boaters find smooth waves. And night vision cameras can help them stay safe. Flir makes what most consider the industry's best marine equipment.

Until recently, all of these businesses have been steady, albeit slow, growers. Revenues were $1.4 billion in 2012, rising to $1.56 billion in 2015.

In 2016, management began to actively seek additional markets for its patented technology. In 2016, sales reached $1.66 billion, an increase of 6.75 percent.

The most important new avenue of business is automotive. Vehicles are more dependent than ever on technology. Cameras have become key. Flir managers are pushing the company's proprietary technology into the marketplace with an embedded system strategy for machine vision.

It's innovative because it puts Flir vision systems into modular components on the edge of the network.

The advantage of edge computing is efficiency. Much of the initial processing occurs where the data is being collected. This reduces demands on the network. It is also much less expensive to produce small board computers and systems on modules.

Recently, Flir released its Spinnaker SDK. The software development kit is available for Tier 1 auto parts suppliers. The plan is to bring Flir's Boson thermal imaging sensor technology to advanced driver assistance systems development at original equipment manufacturers. The technology is currently available only in the aftermarket.

ABI Research predicts annual shipments of night vision systems, including thermal imaging sensors, will swell from 200,000 in 2017 to 4.2 million units by 2021. This is the beginning of the next phase for Flir. When the company breaks into the automotive OEM market, a new door will open. It will also accelerate revenue growth.

HOW TO PLAY: Flir shares were up 30.5 percent in 2017, 125 percent during the past five years through early 2018, and are still buyable for new investors.

A Singular Power Source: Monolithic Power Systems

Michael Hsing has spent his entire professional life in search of a single-chip power solution. For electrical engineers, it is a Holy Grail of sorts: the epitome of efficiency.

By the time Hsing founded **Monolithic Power Systems** (MPWR) in 1997, he was already well known in Silicon Valley. His resume was full of integrated circuit patents and senior job titles at leading firms. However, in 1998, he took the first step toward his lifelong ambition. His fledgling company developed a single chip to power backlighting for notebook computers. At the time, it was a massive technological accomplishment. Mobile computers were more like small briefcases than notebooks. Power-hungry screens, sensors, and processors sapped performance. Hefty batteries were a necessity.

The Monolithic solution was a game changer. By 2003 the tiny company had 40 percent of the market. By 2005, notebooks were changing computing, and 80 percent of them were using Monolithic chips.

Then, at the zenith of Monolithic's early success, Hsing

39

took the company in a new direction. He leveraged the firm's design expertise to diversify. Monolithic began designing chips for the more sophisticated LCD TVs, set-top boxes, and wireless devices that were becoming popular with consumers. Sales and profits surged higher.

In 2009, Monolithic made another critical transition. Although its consumer electronics business accounted for the lion's share of its $165 million annual sales, corporate managers saw a new opportunity emerging. They recognized that semiconductors were being commoditized. Networks were becoming pervasive. Software infrastructure was making networks of connected things possible. That world promised to be a bonanza for the tiny, super-efficient IC chips that Monolithic designed. IC designers began to build new sensors and other products for industrial, data center, telecommunication, and automotive applications.

Then, in 2013, Hsing achieved his lifelong professional ambition. The company he founded patented a monolithic power module that integrated the entire power system into a single package. It was a groundbreaking moment. It was also perfect timing for a world moving toward sensors and connected things.

Since 2013, the compound annual growth rate for Monolithic has been 17.7 percent. Overall margins have risen to 55.7 percent. These metrics put the company far ahead of its competitors. In 2016, sales were $389 million. And it is only beginning.

At a November 30, 2017, investor conference, Bernie Blegen, chief financial officer, laid out the size of the opportunity in networked things, and how the company was positioned to win market share.

Today, cars have an average of $350 worth of semiconductor content. Consumers take for granted their vehicles, which have modern infotainment systems, intelligent electric devices, safe lighting, and advanced driver assistance systems. However, USB charging, heads-up display systems, electric mirrors, seats HVAC systems, and LED light all use sophisticated ICs. And the necessary collection of cameras, radar/LiDar, and ultrasonic sensors for future cars will only increase IC use. All of these will benefit from reduced power consumption.

Monolithic is currently working with every major auto parts supplier in the world. Through the likes of Delphi, Bosch, Panasonic Automotive, Magna, and Mitsubishi Electric, the company can reach end customers such as Ford, Nissan, BMW, Mercedes, GM, Volvo, Toyota, and Volkswagen.

The company is also moving aggressively into eMotion. It developed a gearless IC that is 30 percent more efficient than traditional electric motor setups. It creates less heat while offering more torque. It is more power efficient and less expensive. Ultimately, those savings fall to the bottom line in more substantial profits at value-added resellers and OEMs. Blegen points to a variety of applications including drones, industrial robots, security cameras, printers, and cars. Surgical robots require 78 motors and 180 sensors. The opportunity is worth $20,000 per unit.

And the company is leveraging its design wins in field programmable integrated circuits too. Currently, the market for such intellectual property is $1 billion. It encompasses automotive, wireless, cell towers, enterprise networking and data center servers, point of sale, and connected devices like ATMs, medical devices, and security. All of these subsectors are undergoing an upgrade cycle as they become more connected to the network.

The other significant innovation at Monolithic is delivery. Like most companies, Monolithic has been experimenting with self-service. Recently the company developed an artificial intelligence platform. It gives original equipment manufacturers and value-added resellers a way to buy ICs with no more effort than purchasing printer toner on Amazon.com. The buyer logs in to the Monolithic AI platform and chooses vital metrics. Monolithic uploads the customer design specifics into parts. These can be e-Motion, DC/DC, or AC/DC plug and play modules or ICs. The pieces are shipped to the customer by UPS in a few days. Blegen says there is strong demand for this service. The addressable market is $4 billion, representing $1 billion for ICs and $3 billion for components.

Business momentum is surging. Its new products are gaining market share at a rapid rate because they are best in class. And through mid-2018, the company had $305 million in cash and no debt.

Investors have noted all of this. The underlying common stock has been a big winner. Shares gained 38.1 percent in 2017. From 2012 through April 2018, the shares rose 805 percent. Yet growth still supports the valuation, making the stock still buyable.

Eastman Kodak has become a punch line for the digital era. Investors wonder how a company that invented digital cameras failed so miserably in the digital age. What Kodak managers missed was the applications beyond paper photographs. They were solving the wrong problem.

Optical sensors, microphones, and other measurement sensors have transformed commerce by turning analog events into digital data that can be easily measured, manipulated, and analyzed. And engineers are using those inputs to build tiny, cost-effective satellites, contact lens systems capable of taking pictures, vertical farming, and heavy duty mining rigs that would have been unthinkable a decade ago.

It is not only sensors. They are building blocks, added to awesome computer processing power and data analytic software. The promise is sensors will continue to fall in price.

HOW TO PLAY: Cognex, Flir, and Monolithic Power Systems are attractive longer-term businesses because they have built important competitive advantages. Investors should embrace this. A commoditized business can very quickly become a monopoly with the right managers. Keep in mind, the Rockefeller and Carnegie fortunes were built because low prices (and low margins for new entrants) kept competitors out.

Fast Forward

Sensors are like the eyes, ears, nose, and skin of this digital age. They are helping engineers sense and grasp the world at a much deeper level and at a fast-forward pace. While they are commoditized on the low end, in the middle and high end there is plenty of opportunity for smart, agile companies to profit. Cognex, Flir, and Monolithic Power Systems are a good place to start for investors, as are innovative industrial leaders like Caterpillar, Deere, Rio Tinto, and Billiton that are using these devices to improve and speed up the world's business metabolism.

CHAPTER 3

DECODING THE GENOME: STRETCHING THE MEANING OF LIFE

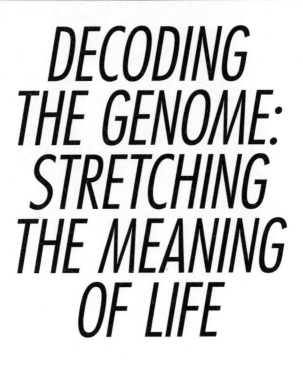

The term *game changer* is often overused. But the Human Genome Project (HGP) was a true game changer for health sciences. In this chapter I will explore how HGP reset the playing field, and why it would not have been possible without advances in computing power. I'll show you some of the mind-bending applications that are now possible because it is possible to edit the building blocks of life. And I will offer insights on two businesses set to capitalize on the longer-term growth of a sector that is only now getting started in a big way.

The Project Begins

In 1990, many of the world's best genetic scientists came together to try to read the complete human genome. The effort was ambitious and unprecedented.

The Human Genome Project was funded initially by the US Department of Energy and the National Institutes of Health. The idea had been the topic of academic debate for years. However, funding from the two prominent US agencies set the wheels into motion. The project gained traction quickly as geneticists from the United States, United Kingdom, France, Australia, and China pooled data and research.

The project was expected to take 15 years. After all, the goal was to map all 3.3 billion pairs of human DNA. Given limited computer power, the magnitude of the challenge was staggering. However, collaboration and advances in information technology fostered innovation. By the mid-1990s, new research in sequence analysis propelled the project closer to completion.

Then, in 1998, Celera Genomics, a public company started by Craig Venter, pushed the envelope.

Catapulted by the large amount of shared data from the HGP, Celera began a private-sector quest to read the genome. Initially, the public and private quests sparked collaboration. Venter started his research at NIH, and he maintained many working relationships.

The amity did not last. Celera ultimately went public. Now it had shareholders who demanded a return on investment. When management decided to seek patents for key parts of its formerly private research, scientists involved with HGP stepped up their efforts. The goal was to keep the completed human genome in the public domain. To make certain this held true, President Bill Clinton declared in March 2000 that the genome sequence could not be patented.

Biotechnology companies' shares plummeted on the news. Around $50 billion of market capitalization evaporated in two trading sessions.

On June 6, 2000, a rough draft of the human genome sequence was completed by public interests. A year later, more refined research papers were jointly published by HGP and Celera in *Nature* and *Science*, respectively. The final HGP version posted on April 14, 2003—years ahead of schedule.

The official cost of the HGP was $3 billion. Ultimately the project covered 92 percent of the human genome sequence. More important, it set a precedent for the world's scientists working together to accomplish a big task. The project also showed that a little competition for a feisty upstart is a good thing.

Researchers discovered humans have 22,300 protein-coding genes. There were many more duplicates than initially believed. And fewer than 7 percent of these are specific to a vertebrate. Humans may rule the animal world, but we are much less unique than we first assumed.

The benefits of the HGP are being revealed in new ways virtually every day. Initially, scientists expected the project would help researchers target specific diseases, identify mutations, and design innovative medications. However, there have been other unintended benefits. Researchers have been able to open new avenues in forensic applied sciences, biofuels, and even agriculture.

Smaller companies are pursuing innovative research in all of these fields today. Their success has been groundbreaking and is now pushing on at a fast-forward pace.

The Death of Aging: Human Longevity Inc.

Slowing the aging process is as important as finding a cure for cancer or cardiovascular disease, according to Venter, now independent and one of the most prominent gene experts in the country. He's right, and it might even be easier.

Besides his pioneering efforts to help decode the human genome, Venter has a long and storied history in the field as both a scientist and entrepreneur. But a primary accomplishment was the work that his firm, **Celera Genomics,** did with the publicly funded Human Genome Project to produce the first draft of the human genome sequence.

At the time, this so-called Book of Life was viewed as the key to unlocking all of the mysteries that had befuddled medical researchers for centuries. The promise seemed immense.

While the accomplishment was thrilling, merely unlocking the genome was ultimately unsatisfying. Venter found that just isolating genes that implied patients would develop terrible diseases was not that much help since a dangerous mutation was not inevitable.

He soon realized that he needed a systematic way to process all of the possible combinations and permutations. And that's where machine learning and super-powerful computing come in. In a subsequent major venture, he helped launch a biosciences start-up called Human Longevity Inc. (HLI). There, Venter began deploying big data analytics across the entirety of a patient's DNA, searching for intricate patterns of interaction.

Although most researchers in the genetics field focused on cancer or cardiovascular disease, his data analysis showed these are not predictable from the genome. Inherited markers play a role in less than 10 percent of cancer, he discovered, as lifestyle choices like diet and exercise are far more predictive for heart-related diseases. However, there is a direct correlation between most cancers, heart disease, and aging. Given this, it made sense for HLI to focus on strategies to delay aging.

That may seem like dreamy logic and, like other genetic researcher firms, HLI is still looking for markers in the human genome that might help eradicate cancer. But Venter is unequivocal that the idea there is a cancer gene is wildly simplistic. Genes serve many functions and cutting one may give rise to unintended consequences for the patient or their progeny.

There is a clear path to delaying degeneration in aging, and it begins with stem cells—the undifferentiated cells that are deployed by the body to repair cellular damage. Studies show that older people have just a tiny fraction of the stem cells found in children. HLI believes it's possible to bank these cells at birth, edit them to correct any later abnormalities, and then return them to the patient later in life as a pick-me-up to rejuvenate disease resistance.

HLI is not the first company led by a visionary pursuing longevity as a panacea. Elizabeth Parrish, the head of BioViva, a small Seattle biotechnology firm, became patient zero for an experimental gene therapy. Alphabet invested as much as $240 million in Calico, a company led by Genentech ex-chief Arthur Levinson. Calico hopes to reverse the aging process. And Martine Rothblatt, head of United Therapeutics, wants to take things one step further by fusing biotechnology with technology. Her plan would allow people to upload the data of their mind into a software program now while the biotechnology catches up. It reminds me of the way the anthropomorphic robots in the British television series "Humans" digitized their memories for later review.

In 2000, when Venter announced the sequencing of the human genome, there was talk about eradicating cancer deaths within a generation. Yet cancer, heart disease, and other age-related diseases still account for two-thirds of deaths.

Eradicating cancer with genomic research alone might be a stretch given what we now know, but delaying aging by just seven years could cut the risk of cancer and heart disease by half. Forecasts like that never get old.

Seeing Is Believing

In 2017, British doctors injected lab-modified DNA into the eyes of a blind man to restore his sight.

The 29-year-old man had retinitis pigmentosa (RP), an inherited eye disorder. Patients suffer a slow deterioration in vision before ultimately losing sight altogether. The condition is the leading cause of blindness among young Britons, and it is irreversible.

At least that used to be the case.

After the human genome was successfully sequenced in 2003, it was just a matter of time before scientists started tinkering with the building blocks of life to fix medical disorders.

RP is the result of a single faulty gene condition: choroideraemia. The defect causes the cells in the retina that detect light to slowly die. The initial symptoms are poor night and peripheral vision as rods deteriorate. Eventually, the cones fail too, leading to the complete loss of central, detailed, and color vision.

In theory, a good copy of a bad gene would fix everything.

Researchers at the NHS, University of Oxford, and Nightstar worked for several years under the guidance of Robert MacLaren, professor of ophthalmology at the University of Oxford. Their lone goal was to develop the therapy that would fix the bad gene.

Tinkering with genetic code is complicated, even with the latest advances in gene editing. Changing one gene often leads to unintended consequences for others. Still, the team persisted.

"Changing the genetic code is always undertaken with great caution, but the new sequence we are using has proven to be highly effective in our laboratory studies," MacLaren told the *Daily Telegraph*.

So far, so good. The first patient went home to recover. The initial results were encouraging, but MacLaren acknowledges it could take several years before there is conclusive evidence that the deterioration has ceased.

Researchers may have already won. Gene therapy is moving out of the labs and into the operating rooms. Patients see real breakthrough results.

The BBC reports a French children's hospital used gene therapy to treat a teenage boy afflicted with sickle cell disease. Researchers modified the genetic instructions in his bone marrow, resulting in the production of healthy red blood cells. After 15 months there is still no sign the disease has returned.

Such results are a game changer for the healthcare business. In addition to offering real hope for the ill, it resets the rules for pharmaceutical and biotechnology companies, healthcare providers, and insurers. They are all moving at fast forward speed to solve big genetic problems.

The Internet in a Shoe Box

Microsoft wants to use synthetic DNA strands to solve the world's data deluge.

Massive data centers are a necessary evil in the current

information technology era. Technology firms are rushing to build the power hungry centers all over the globe. And for good reason: Transforming the analog world to digital is creating ungodly amounts of data from sensors on our bodies and in our cars, our homes, and our offices.

Just try using the Live button on your Facebook status function; you can now broadcast HD video in real-time to the world at any time, and have the expectation the film will live forever. The scope is mind-blowing.

Even more data will come from sources like tractors, grain elevators, jet engines and cockpit computers, street lights, and municipal power systems, which will all be talking to each other. All of it will need to be stored and ready for complex analytics.

In 2015, Cisco Systems estimated that some 50 billion devices would be connected to the Internet by 2020, generating 44 zetabytes, or 44 trillion gigabytes, of data annually.

Finding a way to efficiently store this deluge of data is going to be one of the next great challenges for the tech world.

That's why some engineers have been looking at deoxyribonucleic acid, better known as DNA.

Human DNA is remarkably dense, which makes it super-efficient at storing information. And this DNA is also unstable, which makes it easy to manipulate. Plus, it can remain readable for anywhere from 1,000 to 10,000 years—way longer than any other storage system. That's the perfect mix of attributes for data scientists.

Each DNA strand includes countless combinations of four base chemicals: adenine, cytosine, guanine, and thymine. Biochemists refer to these chemicals by their first letters: A, C, G, and T. Normal computer data consists of 1s and 0s. So, in April 2016, executives at Microsoft purchased 10 million strands of synthetic DNA from a company called Twist Bioscience.

The idea was to test how well digital content could be stored on the organic material. Microsoft first translated the 1s and 0s into a digital DNA sequence of letters. It gave that sequence to Twist and asked them to duplicate it with synthetic DNA. After Twist copied the data, it gave the organic material to Microsoft for testing. Researchers at Microsoft and the University of Washington found that all the data—about 200 megabytes of digital documents, artwork, and a high-resolution music video from the band OK Go!—were intact and retrievable.

Storing digital data on DNA holds tremendous potential because it overcomes all of the shortcomings of current data storage science. It doesn't degrade with exposure to magnetic fields or to extreme temperatures. It's not susceptible to data loss in the event of power loss, which can happen even with state-of-the-art solid-state drive technology. It's long lasting. As long as the medium is kept in a relatively stable state, it can last thousands of years without degradation. In fact, recently discovered wooly mammoth DNA is sufficiently robust to resurrect an animal that has been extinct for 10,000 years.

However, DNA's density ranks as its most impressive attraction as a storage medium. Microsoft was able to store 200 MB of data on a surface about the size of the point of a pencil. Researchers estimate that all of the public data on the Internet would fit in the size of a shoebox. Maybe LeBron James' shoebox, but you get the idea.

There is still one obstacle to overcome before DNA data storage goes mainstream: The process costs too much, even for Microsoft. Researchers are working on reducing the expense. And the cost has been falling for encoding and decoding digital data to and from synthetic DNA. Hopefully, as research continues, new processes will lead to savings.

> **HOW TO PLAY:** Like other cloud computing companies, Microsoft is riding a wave that is expecting to create a massive amount of new data. Even as the Redmond software company competes to build new data centers, it's working on the science to make them obsolete. This is a brave new era of innovation. This is one reason why Microsoft shares are still in the conversation for investors. Keep it on your radar.

DNA in the Oil Patch

Biota Technologies is doing something that has never been done before. It's using DNA sequencing to help US shale oil and gas producers slash the cost of oil production.

Shale producers need help. Saudi Arabia and other OPEC members want to put them out of business by flooding the market with cheap oil, keeping prices so low they can't make money.

DNA sequencing is a game changer.

Understanding the building blocks of life was supposed to allow researchers providence to construct groundbreaking new treatments and precision therapies.

It is kind of what Biota is doing. It's using all of the advances made in DNA sequencing and some sophisticated data analytic software to find the very best places to drill new oil wells.

Currently, old science underlies most US shale exploration. Microseismic, petrophysical, and geochemistry technologies are designed for finding conventional and offshore oil. Shale production is a different beast entirely.

It involves poking holes in the ground; injecting high-pressure mixtures of water, sand, and chemicals to fracture the shale layer to release trapped oil; and hoping wells have been arranged appropriately to capture the windfall.

Ajay Kshatriya, chief executive and cofounder of Biota, believes subsurface DNA diagnostics can help. Clever application of math and science aside, the idea seems simple enough.

Rock shavings are recollected from the wellhead, and DNA microbe samples are extracted. From there, DNA sequencing and data analytics are used to model the subsurface depth, size, and shape of the oil reservoir. Ultimately, the goal of the model is to enable better placement of future wells for capture.

"This is a whole new way of measuring these wells and, by extension, sucking out more oil for less," says Kshatriya.

It could not come at a more opportune time for US shale producers. *Reuters* reports they slashed costs by 50 percent over the two years prior to 2018 to stave off OPEC attacks. Although the cartel has been friendlier lately, there is no telling how long that will last.

While Biota will not say precisely how much its technology will cost, Kshatriya claims it should not exceed 1 percent of the total cost to bring a new well entirely online. According to a March 2016 report from US Department of Energy, that ranges from $5 million to $8 million, depending on location and geology.

So far the company has been involved in about 80 wells, primarily in North Dakota and Texas. And big players like Statoil ASA and EP Energy have nothing but good things to say.

J. C. Wan, the geophysical advisor at EP Energy, told *CEP Magazine*: "The DNA Diagnostics tool is being used to address real unmet challenges in our Permian Basin fields. The early results are promising, and if DNA sequencing can be proven to work, it would be a game changer for our company and the industry."

When the HGP was completed in 2003, I doubt anyone would have bet its building blocks would be used for oil exploration. Fourteen years later, there is a genuine possibility the science will help save the US shale business and tens of thousands of jobs.

For investors, the best strategy is to buy the companies that provide the equipment and services to help smaller companies move through the process. Let's check some out.

Digitizing the Drug Development Process: IQVIA Holdings

While **IQVIA Holdings** (IQV) may not have the prettiest of names, its business is rock solid. The North Carolina company is cornering the lucrative market of managing drug company clinical trials.

The cost of drug development is mind-bending. Networks of physicians and investigators must be assembled. Patients need to be recruited. Regulatory submissions must be filed. Safety protocols have to be designed, implemented, and monitored. And the data needs to be collected and analyzed.

Collecting all of the blood work alone is a Herculean task.

Research from Battelle, a global science and technology research organization, found the cost per participant ranged from $36,500 to $42,000. Some trials can have tens of thousands of participants. In 2013, 1,148,340 people were participating.

It's a massive business that pharmaceutical companies are all too willing to outsource.

In 2016, a company called Quintiles merged with a rival, IMS. In addition to creating the biggest company in the sector, it was a masterstroke. Alone, the companies were strong; but together, they are a powerhouse.

IMS catalogs 780,000 streams of healthcare data, taken from 45 billion transactions per year. Anonymous medical records, diagnoses, prescriptions, and even blood test information are collected, analyzed, and monetized.

The Quintiles legacy business built a substantial research and development franchise.

The merger took these assets to the next level. The combined company, IQVIA, is using advances in information technology to mix in real-time social media monitoring, customer relationship management, data analytics, and its domain expertise.

Its Next-Generation clinical offering is already winning business from companies with no previous relationships. During an August 2017 analyst conference call, Ari Bousbib, chief executive, said the company had secured $600 million in new business since the merger, based on the new product.

The enthusiasm pushed the backlog to an estimated $9.99 billion as of the end of June. The company expects to convert $3 billion during the next 12 months.

And more good news is likely.

According to Bousbib, the Food and Drug Administration has signaled a policy change to support more innovation. This will streamline regulations and lead to more trials.

IQVIA is pressing ahead, too. It's now investing heavily to leverage its position as the premier contract research organization in the sector. In 2017, its Master Data Management platform was to be integrated with Salesforce.com, a popular marketing platform.

All of this comes at a time when advances in science and IT are making drug discovery easier. Dramatic increases in compute power, coupled with better modeling and the introduction of artificial intelligence, are leading to medical breakthroughs.

HOW TO PLAY: Immunotherapy and precision medicine, innovative drug delivery strategies made possible by the Human Genome Project, should bring a lot of new drugs to trials.

Investors have noticed. IQV shares rose 125 percent at a steady pace from 2013 through January 2018, including a 28.73 percent gain in 2017 alone. It's still buyable for newcomers.

Sequencing at a New Level: Illumina Inc.

On paper, precision medicine seems ideal: Tailor medical treatment to a patient's genetic make-up.

To make this reality, researchers will need cost-effective DNA sequencing provided by **Illumina Inc**. (ILMN). The San Diego company has taken a leadership role in genotyping, sequencing, gene expression, and proteomics. And its future could not be brighter.

Most patients currently diagnosed with cancer undergo a battery of oncology tests and usually end up with chemotherapy. That one-size-fits-all treatment carpet bombs everything, killing good and bad cells indiscriminately.

Precision medicine is more of a smart bomb. Doctors locate the mutation at the cellular level and find the specific drug treatment to correct the abnormality. Then they calibrate the dosage based on personal genetics.

The theory is great. The only holdback is cost.

In 2014, Illumina used powerful cloud-based computers and proprietary hardware to command 70 percent of the sequencing market. It pushed the cost from $44,000 in 2010, to just $1,000 per genome. The time required shrank to less than a week, making it cost effective for almost every patient.

For perspective, sequencing the first human genome took 13 years, and costs swelled to $3 billion.

The massive price decline is important. It is keeping competitors out of the business. There is no margin. When contenders have popped up, Illumina has swallowed them whole. In 2011, it acquired Epicenter Biotechnologies. When French pharmaceutical giant Hoffman LaRoche made an unsolicited $5.4 billion offer for Illumina, managers wisely rejected the advance outright. Since that time the share price has risen sixfold.

When the company reported third-quarter financial results in October 2017, sales rose 17 percent year over year to $714 million. Its newest sequencer, NovaSeq, shipped 80 units during the last 90 days, bringing the total to 200 through three quarters. Francis deSouza, the CEO, has repeatedly told analysts they should adjust their financial models significantly above earlier guidance.

Given what is at stake, the strong growth makes sense. Recently the FDA approved KYMRIAH, the very first immune cell therapy. There are 1,000 such drugs in clinical trials in the United States alone. Genome research centers, pharmaceutical companies, academic institutions, clinical research organizations, and biotechnology companies are racing to make discoveries and develop drug treatments. They all require sequencers.

Another important market is rare and undiagnosed diseases. In November, insurance giant **UnitedHealth Group** (UNH) began covering some sequencing in such cases. Illumina executives believe 100 million people will be affected. This market largely did not exist a year ago.

Illumina shares rose 35.2 percent in 2017 and were up 334 percent in the five years prior to 2018. The shares are still buyable for newcomers.

When the HGP was completed in 2003, few people could have imagined all of the possible applications of understanding the building blocks of human life. As computer power, storage, and data analytics have progressed, scientists have pushed the limits of health sciences. Venter, a key player in the HGP, is working to end aging as we know it. English researchers have used gene editing to cure blindness. Doctors in Texas used it to help a fetus afflicted with spina bifida. Engineers have even used DNA sequencing to find oil and gas in North Dakota.

The world of biotechnology is shifting into overdrive. The HGP has opened new fields and led to countless innovations. This should be a golden era for investors, though investing in new drug discovery has always been hit and miss.

In 2000, excitement was running at a fevered pitch. Celera was getting close to a full sequence of the human genome. The promise of new drugs and cheaper discovery helped the biotechnology stocks soar. Then the Clinton Administration stepped in and erased that $50 billion in market capitalization.

And there are other risks. Despite HGP, drug discovery is still very time consuming and expensive. A study published in *Nature Reviews Drug Discovery* in 2010 found the average cost for a new drug is $1.8 billion.

Even then, getting the drug to market is not assured. Most new drugs do not gain approval from the Food and Drug Administration.

HOW TO PLAY: I have focused on infrastructure investments. While the genetics sector is young, long-term winners are being born right now. Most are too small to have established track records that give us comfort as investors. In contrast, IQVIA Holdings and Illumina Inc. have been around and proven their worth, and hold important competitive advantages.

Fast Forward

Determining the human genome two decades ago put scientists on the path toward solving some of the greatest medical problems of our time. Biotech companies and their partners in the medical device industry have harnessed vast new computing power, the cloud, and artificial intelligence to push the fast forward button on therapeutic discoveries. While companies making new drugs tend to be hit or miss for investors, buying the shares of the biomedical equipment makers, data analysts, and robotics makers like Iqvia Holdings and Illumina has been proven effective.

CHAPTER 4

BIG DATA: MAKING SENSE OF IT ALL

Retailers have been collecting digital exhaust for years—the voluminous data tracks consumers leave behind as they navigate the connected world. Now called "*big data*," these vapor trails are extremely valuable if captured and manipulated adeptly, as they fit neatly between sensor proliferation, massive computer processing power, and next-generation analytics software.

In this chapter I will track the rise of big data. I will show how it has informed decision making at retailers, hospitals, and investment managers. And I will tell you how a couple of little known businesses are building foundational franchises in this fast growing and very important niche.

Harvesting Big Data

Andrew Pole is not a household name.

He is a data scientist. He is also the senior manager of media and database marketing at Target Corp., the second largest discount retailer in the United States.

In 2010, at the Predictive Analytics World conference in Washington, DC, he made a startling admission about the use of data at Target. At the time, the Minneapolis company was the fifth largest discount retailer. But it was growing fast. Under Pole, the company was designing and implementing complex data mining strategies. It was pulling information from numerous sources and using analytics to target and push specific shoppers to their stores.

Newborns are money guzzlers. Retailers know this. New and expectant parents are coveted because they are likely to spend $5,000 a year for baby supplies. Pole built a system to find these people *before* childbirth.

For 47 minutes, he told fellow data scientists at the Washington conference about the system Target employed. He explained how data was scraped from e-mail click-throughs, online browsing and cookies, mobile IDs and coupons, social media, credit cards, and barcode scans. He admitted that it sounded like Big Brother, but promised it was entirely legal and necessary to build actionable profiles.

Finding expectant parents through baby registries was easy. In the parlance of data scientists, it was a "known known." And the company promptly began target marketing to that sample with e-mails, mobile coupons, and direct mail. However, the true test of its data mining operation was finding evidence of "known unknowns." These are connections that might exist, but had not been proved.

For example, company research showed, when a woman of childbearing years began to switch from scented to unscented lotions, it was a dead giveaway she might be pregnant. Later back testing revealed that women in their second trimester began buying cotton balls and washcloths at a ferocious rate.

All of this information was valuable and actionable. Target ramped up marketing efforts to secure future sales with offers for baby cribs, clothing, diapers, rattles, and all of the other effects that separate new parents from their money.

There were surprises embedded in the data, too. These were "unknown unknowns," the kinds of connection the data scientists would have never expected. When men purchased diapers, for example, they were also likely to purchase beer.

Pole's Target experiment was early but effective data science. He determined his objective, found a way to collect the right data, and set a strategy to define success. His team became a big part of the growth story at Target. Their prowess with data was a legitimate competitive advantage that would not have been possible a decade earlier.

It was also a watershed moment in big data. It showed the importance of collecting and understanding data. It revealed that plenty of actionable intelligence is embedded in data that looks like noise. The key is finding the tools to see and analyze it.

Almost a decade later, the world has changed again.

Data growth is accelerating. It's more detailed, and it is coming from everywhere. Harnessing that data has the potential to change healthcare, business, finance, and social structures throughout the world.

Making Sense of Big Data

In 2003, researchers at the University of California at Berkeley determined that all of the measurable data created in the world to that point amounted to five billion gigabytes (GB). One year later, the world created another five billion GB of data. By 2010, that amount was being created every two days. Three years later, the period shrunk to just 10 minutes.

Data scientists believe that by 2020, worldwide data volumes will reach 40 zettabytes, that is, 40 with 21 zeroes. It is a number almost too big to comprehend, but think of it in these terms: Imagine all of the grains of sand in the world today. Take into account all of the 23 major deserts and all of the coastal and inland shorelines. Then multiply that number by 75.

We are recording more data than ever before.

In the mainframe era of the 1970s, early computer workers started the process in a rudimentary way. Documents, financial reports, stock records, personal files, and other sources were manually collected. Then they were fed into large relational databases where the results were digitized. It was a lengthy process. The Internet changed the input method. Networks, powered by end users submitting queries, began to create data on their own. Then developers started to connect machines to networks, creating even more digital data.

As the volume surged, databases that relied on a single processor quickly became overwhelmed.

In 2003, Doug Cutting and Mike Cafarella created Hadoop, a collection of open-source software utilities inspired by a Google white paper about distributed file systems. It changed everything.

The idea was simple: Instead of taking the data to a central processor, Hadoop used the distributed power of networked computers. The data was spread across many processors, on many connected servers and clusters. It was robust, scalable, and it automatically compensated for hardware failures at the application level.

In 2004, Map Reduce, another Google innovation, helped developers easily map the data over multiple servers, while simultaneously reducing workloads. Suddenly, there was a way to store and segment digitized data at scale. The official launch of Amazon Web Services in 2006 gave developers access to pay-as-you go compute and storage at reasonable costs.

A new set of digital data entrepreneurs, and their enterprises, were born.

In the past, great thinkers thought about problems. They recorded their observations in white papers that were peer reviewed. Consensus formed. It became knowledge.

Big data flips that idea on its head. Sensors, networks, and cloud computing have allowed researchers to collect massive amounts of information. They're building software tools to see patterns, stories, and actionable intelligence that previously were scarcely imagined, much less implemented. It is a new form of knowledge with unexplored potential.

Jay Walker

Jay Walker is a serial inventor and the cofounder of TEDMED Foundation, the organization that runs the popular TEDMED annual conference focusing on advancement in health and medicine.

In an interview for *The Face of Big Data*, a 2016 PBS documentary, Walker likens big data to the invention of the microscope in the 1650s, only bigger. Just as the microscope allowed researchers to see cells and bacteria that nobody thought existed, big data, coupled with software, is allowing the next generation of innovators to see into the world of unknown patterns and relationships.

He has some experience. In addition to being the lead inventor for 943 US patents, Walker also founded Priceline. com in 1998. The online aggregator of hotel room inventories and airline tickets turned hidden pricing relationships in the hospitality industry into a $105 billion business and fantastic shareholder wealth.

On any given day, hotels and airlines have unused capacity. They earn nothing by leaving rooms or seats unfilled. However, it is also not in their interest to advertise excess capacity. The laws of supply and demand would reduce prices and discourage patrons from prebooking.

Priceline.com exploited the hidden relationship between excess capacity and advertised hospitality pricing.

> **HOW TO PLAY:** Shares of the company, now known as **Booking Holdings** (BKNG), have enjoyed a 15-year compound average rate of return of 42 percent. That means, on average, the stock has doubled every two years since 2004.

Marc Andreessen

Marc Andreessen is another Internet pioneer with sky-high expectations for big data.

Andreessen was just 24 when Netscape, the company he

cofounded soon after grad school, became a public company. In 1999, the web browser business was sold to AOL for $4.2 billion. Since that time, he has been a successful venture investor.

In 2016, Andreessen told *Vox Media* that he believed digitalization and big data would lead to entrepreneurs finally solving the problem of escalating healthcare and education costs. He pointed to the precedent set in retailing. Digitalization led to lower prices and better service for consumers. Robotics did the same for manufacturing.

"How audacious is it to think you could bring tech to healthcare or education?," he told the *Vox Media* reporter, Timothy B. Lee.

Disrupting healthcare alone would be a game changer. According to research from the Centers for Medicare and Medicaid Services, in 2016, health spending accounted for 17.9 percent of gross domestic product. Spending grew 4.3 percent annually, well above both inflation and GDP growth. It is a big problem that policymakers are desperate to curb.

Digitization and big data analytics hit the problem head-on. Turning mountains of medical information into digital data is efficient. Exposing that data to pattern recognition software is certain to lead to even greater cost savings.

McKinsey & Co., the global consulting group, estimates that making sense of that data will be worth $450 billion annually.

Ultimately, that number may look like a rounding error compared to the potential cost savings. Better data analysis helps doctors make faster, more accurate diagnosis. The use of evidence-based medicine eliminates unneeded tests. It also helps healthcare organizations exchange medical records and deliver more personalized treatments. Faster and better is critical, when time is money.

In a 2013 research report, "The Big Data Revolution in US Health Care: Accelerating Value and Innovation," McKinsey analysts point to the HealthConnect software network at Kaiser Permanente, an integrated managed care consortium in Oakland, California. Kaiser uses HealthConnect to facilitate data exchange and digital medical records across all of its facilities. It has already led to savings of $1 billion.

More importantly, Kaiser has become a model for integrated healthcare providers. The company invested $6 billion in its Electronic Health Record system with the express goal of cutting costs by slowing the pace of readmissions, the most expensive part of healthcare.

In Washington state, that meant engaging patients with automated voice mail, e-mail, online reminders, and more. The goal was to have patients involved with their follow-up screenings, lab tests, medications, and appointments. Disease, complex case, and transition management teams all play a role in keeping costs low. All teams are informed and run using automated big data pattern recognition systems.

A Small-Town Hospital Takes Big Data to Heart

It's an approach Geisinger Health Systems has taken to heart.

Danville, Pennsylvania, seems on the surface like every rural town of 5,000. Nestled alongside the winding Susquehanna River, there is a Dunkin' Donuts and three churches: Trinity Methodist, Shiloh United, and St. Joseph's. There is a hardware store and a Chinese buffet.

There is also a cutting-edge medical company trying to remake healthcare with big data.

The reach of Geisinger Health System extends far beyond its picturesque hometown. The company serves three million residents in 45 counties in northeastern Pennsylvania and southern New Jersey. The company has grown in 10 years from two hospitals to twelve, with 30,000 employees and 1,600 full-time physicians. It has become a thought leader in the next era of healthcare. Today, its genomics, precision medicine, and big data initiatives are considered industry templates.

In 2015, Geisinger implemented Unified Data Architecture (UDA), a cutting-edge information technology platform using innovative big data mining. UDA takes digital record keeping to the extreme.

Geisinger was among the first in the country to adopt the Electronic Health Record system. In 1996, EHR was the most powerful tool available. Today it is wholly insufficient. With smartphone penetration pervasive, there is a new set of data available to be mined for actionable intelligence. Patients leave digital data everywhere they interact, from grocery store loyalty programs to smartphone applications. With the appropriate permissions, Geisinger IT engineers learned that great things were possible.

UDA can track, analyze, and correlate a patient's genomic sequence with their ongoing care in real time. It can take data from the patient's smartwatch and smartphone. It can analyze unstructured data like handwritten notes and free-text imaging reports. It can scan 200 million reports in less than one second. UDA is powerful. Researchers believe it will materially change the efficacy of healthcare and its cost structure.

In an article posted to the *Harvard Business Review* in 2016, Alistair Erskine, Bipin Karunakaran, and Jonathan Slotkin explained how UDA has become especially useful in the early detection and treatment of sepsis. The blood infection can be deadly. Having all of the patient information in one place with UDA, including lab results, medications, and vital signs, provides an overarching picture that helps care providers make more informed choices. It also speeds up early detection.

The system is smart enough to analyze the impact of real-time data like blood pressure measurements. It also uses intermediate, ongoing blood culture results data and the impact of antibiotics. The authors found providers using UDA were more than twice as likely to adhere to the correct medical protocol. All of these things are good news for patients.

The UDA is also helping hospitals to reduce surgical costs. The system integrates the surgical supply chain. By tracking everything from sponges, medications, and devices used during surgeries, it is possible to begin to develop protocols to predetermine likely costs. This borrows a page from the lean manufacturing processes that revolutionized the automobile manufacturing. The goal is to reduce waste, cut down inventory, and improve productivity.

It is working. In fiscal 2016, Geisinger logged $129 million in income on $5.5 billion in revenue. As a nonprofit, physician-led entity, Geisinger measures its execution based on how much it is able to offer patients. On that measure, it is winning. The company put millions back into the Pennsylvania and New Jersey communities it serves.

Geisinger was also able to provide $580 million in community benefits, while employing 44,000 people and embarking upon $284 million in capital projects.

The scale of Geisinger is not something most would expect from a small town in Pennsylvania. However, big data, married to powerful cloud-computing platforms, is not bound to geography. The secret is the data, and the way IT professionals can build systems to harness its power.

GE Pioneers Industrial Data

General Electric is in the midst of a remarkable transformation. Slowly but surely, it's moving into the digital world.

What GE is doing amounts to self-preservation. Its financial, infrastructure, and industrial businesses are growing slowly. So it's embracing the future now, before being disrupted by rivals that are fleeter of foot. It's becoming a big data analytics company.

In 2011, Jeffrey Immelt, the chief executive officer, hired Bill Ruh to run a new business, GE Digital. Ruh was tasked with merging the physical and digital worlds and reshaping entire industries with big data analytics.

Ruh immediately began building Predix, the very first cloud-based data analytics platform for the industrial world. It's based on the idea of virtualization. GE calls its concept Digital Twins.

These are digital replicas of actual machinery running in the physical world.

These machines could be real-world jet engines, oil rigs, diagnostic medical equipment, or even entire electric plants. They are outfitted with sensors that constantly upload data to the digital twin software model in the cloud. From there, the data is subjected to powerful pattern recognition tools and analytics.

Writing in *Forbes* in June 2017, Randy Bean, chief executive officer at New Vantage Partners, and Thomas Davenport, a Professor at Babson College, put it succinctly: "The digital twin model can then be used to diagnose faults and predict the need for maintenance, ultimately reducing or eliminating unplanned downtime in that machine."

In 2015, an Accenture report, "Industrial Internet Insights," found that up to 90 percent of companies surveyed believed that big data analytics was either the top priority for the company, or in the top three. There is an urgency to move forward, and quickly.

GE began making investments in the industrial Internet of Things long ago. In 2011, the company announced the acquisition of SmartSignal, a supervised learning business. The 2016 purchase of Wise.io completed the loop with unsupervised learning and modeling.

The acquisitions allowed GE Digital to have its software models learn from training datasets and from hidden patterns in large groupings of data.

The first guinea pig was GE. Since 2013, Predix has been deployed at the company. In 2015 GE said it saved $500 million. Ruh is expecting annual savings to reach $1 billion by 2020.

As a stand-alone business, GE Digital logged $6 billion in sales in 2015 optimizing the production of jet engines, wind turbines, and oil drilling equipment. Ultimately, sales are expected to hit $15 billion by 2020, as the platform is fleshed out with more services and pushed toward more geographies.

In 2016, the company struck a deal with Huawei, China's largest network hardware maker. If Predix is going to reshape the industrial world, it needs to be in the belly of the industrial beast.

It has had some early success. The industrial city of Tianjin, with its nascent "smart city" ambitions, uses Predix to control lampposts. China Airlines and China Telecom use the software to reduce costs. The potential is huge. Although China is the most important manufacturing center in the world, its plants and businesses are among the least modern.

In 2017, internal GE research suggested that industrial data analytics spending in the region will reach $166 billion by 2020. That is a healthy portion of the worldwide expenditure forecast of $500 billion.

It is a big market with immense implications. Virtualization means it is possible to monitor and diagnose the readiness of objects in the physical world in order to optimize performance. Imagine knowing when a jet engine was likely to fail. Technicians could perform preventative maintenance with minimal downtime.

Prognostics would be easier. Using failure data from the digital twin, coupled with historical inputs, engine architects would be empowered to create better designs.

In short, big data is coming to manufacturing. And it will dramatically improve productivity.

Big Data Meets Big Minds

What do big data, cutting edge supercomputers, and sunny days have in common? If you answered the Medallion hedge fund at Renaissance Technologies, give yourself a gold badge.

Gold badges are more than a keepsake at Medallion. A November 2016 *Bloomberg* article, "Inside a Money Making Machine Like No Other," by Katherine Burton, tells the story of the secretive New York hedge fund.

Since 1988 it has racked up annual returns close to 80 percent before fees.

Founded by billionaire mathematician James Simons, the fund blazed a trail in big data before it was a buzzword in Silicon Valley or corporate boardrooms. It hired eccentric geniuses, built powerful, bespoke supercomputers, and wrote innovative algorithms. Then it began looking for patterns in what looked like chaos.

Through mid-2017, the quantitative hedge fund was run by ex-IBM executives Peter Brown and Robert Mercer. Virtually every individual on its 300-person payroll is a scientist. Fully 90 percent have PhDs. And every one of them has a stake in the fund.

Check that: Employees are now the *only* investors.

MIT Sloan School of Management finance professor Andrew Lo believes the strength of the fund is its collection of employees. "Renaissance is the commercial version of the Manhattan Project," he told *Bloomberg*. "They are the pinnacle of quant investing. No one else is even close."

Returns bear this out. Medallion is reported to have earned $55 billion in profits over its 28-year lifespan. More amazing, the fund regularly rolls back capital by distributing profits every six months. Because Medallion makes short-term investments in equities, Brown and Mercer like to keep no more than $10 billion on hand.

In 1993, Renaissance stopped accepting new money altogether.

Many of the best hedge funds charge fees amounting to 3 percent of capital and 20 percent of profits. For its legacy external investors, Medallion charges 5 percent and 44 percent.

It refuses to hire anyone with previous Wall Street experience. Instead, Medallion hires scientists doing exciting work in pattern recognition. Simons himself once worked as a master code breaker at the Institute of Defense Analysis. Many of the first employees worked on early linguistics programming at IBM.

Brown, one such veteran, explained to a *Bloomberg* reporter the importance of finding patterns where none seem to exist: "Big data changes what is possible. It allows scientists to see patterns in what previously looked like chaos. In the case of Renaissance Technologies, the result has been untold riches. Its portfolio managers literally have an unfair advantage over other managers because they are able to see paths more clearly, and invest accordingly."

Visualizing the Digital Path

Right now, companies small and large are building software to visualize, virtualize, and make sense of the digital trail left behind by smartphones, the Internet, commercial and industrial sensors, and wider networks of connected things that will power future smart cars and cities.

The opportunity is unprecedented.

The entire planet is swimming in deep lakes of data. Much of it is unstructured, unused, and ignored. Stories of legacy hardware at hospitals and factories that dump this digital gold are more the norm than the exception.

In other cases, corporations are overwhelmed by the incoming data. Because they are not capable of processing the information, it passes straight through enterprises as a form of digital exhaust.

Almost a decade after Andrew Pole, only 5 percent of retail loyalty card data is mined.

For smart, focused companies, this is the opportunity of a lifetime. It stretches across every sector.

Bringing Developers Out of the Dark: Splunk

For a long time, corporations have been in the dark with their data. It was hopeless.

Splunk (SPLK) is all about visualization. It is the way out.

The San Francisco company was born in 2003, when three friends—Erik Swan, Michael Baum, and Rob Das—had a bright idea. Although the dot-com stock bubble had burst, the growth of Internet traffic was exploding. Corporations were rushing to build virtual homesteads.

Beyond the obvious bandwidth bottlenecks, a new problem was developing for IT professionals. Data coming from the Internet was hyperlinked and searchable. Server side data was not. In many cases, there was no linkage.

Sifting through server logs to fix problems was tedious and expensive.

Das, now chief software architect at Splunk, compared the process to fumbling around—like spelunking in a dark cave. That is how the company got its weird name. Its reputation was built through the next two years as Das and his small team of developers built best-in-class tools for server search.

Splunk 1.0 was released December 2005. Splunk Server was available as a free download. Splunk Professional, a software license aimed at IT pros, was $2,500 for 500 MB setups, and $10,000 for 10 GB.

That was 13 years ago.

Today, Splunk Enterprise Server is a full cloud-based platform. It's a hub where clients can funnel their data. It still does search, but that is now only a feature. The focus is virtualization. In the era of big data, streaming in from multiple channels, clients are more interested in seeing patterns within their datasets and performing analytics. Enterprise Server is full of real-time data, dashboards, charts, and 3D visualizations.

Giving information visual shape and scale makes it more understandable. It makes the data measurable and quantifiable. It also helps developers quickly see connections and relationships that might otherwise go unnoticed. Splunk product managers want to give IT pros all of the tools they need to interpret data, derive insights, and spot potential breaches.

Data security has become more important than ever. In September 2017, Equifax, a consumer credit reporting agency, revealed that a data breach exposed the personal information of 145 million US adults. In September 2016, Yahoo!, an Internet service company, announced that hackers had gained access to more than one billion personal accounts.

Splunk has carefully cultivated relationships with cyber security providers. Enterprise Server allows clients to simply bolt on software from a number of providers. In 2016, Splunk strengthened its ties with cyber security specialists **Symantec**, **Palo Alto Networks**, **ForeScout**, and **Proofpoint**. The companies began integrating their software with Adaptive Response network, a Splunk-led initiative to standardize cyber security architectures.

In February 2018, Splunk acquired Phantom Cyber Corp., a start-up focused on providing rapid, automated responses to security threats. The $350 million acquisition will be weaved into the Adaptive Response network, reinforcing Enterprise Server as the nerve center for big, forward-looking enterprises.

IDC estimates spending for cyber security software will rise to $101.6 billion by 2020. That is an increase of 38 percent over the $73.7 billion spent in 2016.

And that is just for cyber security. Enterprise Server is a hub. The software is being used to visualize data across enterprise applications and IT operations.

In 2017, Aflac, FedEx, Dell EMC, Jiffy Lube, and Papa

John's signed new agreements with Splunk, bringing total subscriptions to 13,000. All of the company's revenue is comprised of licenses, maintenance, and service agreements. This revenue is recurring. That is a very different business model than a traditional one-time sale model. It gives the company revenue visibility. It provides capital to carefully invest in future software to maintain its leadership role.

In March 2018, the company was named in the 2017 Leaders Category of the IDC Marketscape Asia/Pacific Big Data and Analytics Platform Vendor report. It was also named Network-World Asia Big Data and Business Analytics category winner for the third consecutive year.

Its best-in-class software is resonating with customers. In fiscal 2018, the company had total revenues of $1.27 billion, up 34 percent year over year. Total billings surged 38 percent to $1.55 billion.

Splunk is winning because its software provides a trusted turnkey solution. It is not open source; it is stubbornly proprietary. It is like Microsoft Office in a world of free online word processor and spreadsheet software packages. Even Adaptive Response network is more strong-armed than collaborative.

For investors, this is an important distinction. It means a competitive advantage with high margins and pricing power. As the data deluge accelerates, corporations are likely to become more dependent on the visualization tools Splunk provides.

Chinese "Data Farms" Growing Rapidly: GDS Holdings

GDS Holdings (GDS) has a different take on big data. The company does not make visualization software. It does not even do the complex analytics that helps developers make sense of mountains of data.

The story is more about collection and the incredible data explosion expected in China.

GDS Holdings is a fast-growing Shanghai data center business. Founded in 2006 by William Wei Huang, and listed on the New York Stock Exchange in 2016, its outlook could not be brighter.

GDS could be one of the best ways to participate in China's booming tech economy.

China's time has finally come. For two decades political and economic scholars have been forecasting its ascendency to superpower status. This now seems assured. As the United States withdraws and Europe fractures, China is carefully stepping in and picking up the pieces.

President Xi Jinping, the popular leader of the Communist Party of China, is investing heavily in the fixed assets. The country is in the midst of a massive, longer-term economic stimulus program. Roads, bridges, power plants, and data centers are planned all over the country. *Reuters* reports that infrastructure investment rose 9.2 percent year over year, blowing past even the most optimistic forecasts.

In 2005, the Chinese began an ambitious program called Skynet. The goal was to blanket every urban center with all-seeing cameras. By October 2015, *China Daily* reported that the program had completed 100 percent coverage of Beijing, the largest city.

According to a June 2017 report in the *Wall Street Journal*, the number of surveillance cameras throughout the country reached 170 million. Facial recognition software is so widely accepted, it is used to log into mobile apps, gain access to office buildings, and withdraw cash from bank machines. The government is collecting all of this information and adding it to a massive database.

It's being mined with data analytics. Powerful new artificial intelligence software tools are compensating for low light, bad angles, and even aging. And what public cameras don't capture, state-financed bots crawling pervasive social media do.

All of this data is being collected and stored forever in data centers like the ones owned by GDS.

During the October 2017 earnings conference call of US tractor maker Caterpillar, Jim Umpleby, the chief executive officer, noted that new data center construction led to robust demand for its excavators and heavy equipment. Although anecdotal, the comments should be taken in the context of China's larger plans.

The Chinese government is in the process of building the infrastructure for a next-generation surveillance state. GDS is in the business of building, managing, and providing cloud services to data centers.

In November 2017, the company reported that third-quarter service revenues grew 58.5 percent year over year to $77.83 million. Sequential growth was 27.6 percent. Adjusted earnings surged 71.4 percent over the same period the prior year. And commitments to build new data centers increased 41.3 percent to 82,850 square meters.

The company had 496 data center customers through mid-2018, including **Alibaba** (BABA), **Baidu** (BIDU), Tencent, Huawei, Aliyun.com, and others. In October, GDS secured a $100 million investment from **CyrusOne** (CONE), a Texas-based data center services company with 900 customers. Together, the companies will have global reach and local expertise.

The partnership comes at an opportune time. With 1.3 billion citizens, demand for cloud-based services in China is already brisk. This is certain to accelerate as local companies adopt the data-thirsty analytics and Internet of Things strategies more common in the West. And the CyrusOne deal will bring new demand from foreign companies seeking market access.

Technavio, an IT research firm, predicts Chinese data centers will expand at a 13 percent compound annual growth rate over the next four years. The bulk of new projects will be concentrated among only a few players with a foothold in the Shanghai and Beijing markets.

That sounds a lot like GDS.

There is also the nationwide buildout of a surveillance program that will eventually collect facial recognition data for every Chinese man, woman, and child. This is a very ambitious technological challenge that will require a massive investment in new, high-density data centers.

HOW TO PLAY: GDS is winning because it is one of only a handful of companies that has been ordained to build and manage data centers in China. This ensures longer-term profitability and strong margins. It's another example of the way big data has led to big opportunities and big profits.

Fast Forward

When Andrew Pole began speaking at a data science trade conference seven years ago, the field was in its infancy. There was so much data, so much potential and excitement. For the people in the room, it must have felt like the beginning of something really big.

Today, big data is exploding. It is being propelled by the rapid expansion of cloud computing and massive computer processing power. Data scientists have virtually unlimited access to supercomputers and vastly improved analytic software. It is easier than ever to find patterns in seemingly random stacks of data. Naturally, giddy data scientists are using all of these new tools to build better mousetraps, and they are solving really big problems.

Better, more efficient hospitals and drug development are only the beginning.

Splunk and GDS Holdings are foundational businesses. Splunk builds the software that helps developers see patterns in data. It is in the needle-in-a-haystack operation. The developer community has enthusiastically embraced its tools, and that is a very large competitive advantage. GDS is building a network of data centers in China, the most lucrative data market in the world. Investors should focus on those companies whose long-term outlooks will improve with the growth of data.

CHAPTER 5

PREDICTIVE ANALYTICS: THE END OF HIT OR MISS

For most of the industrial age, entrepreneurs have flown by the seat of their pants. They imagined a disruptive new idea, funded it, created it, gussied it up with some branding, and then launched it in public to see if it caught on. This process led to some spectacular products—and plenty of duds. Now, pay-as-you-go supercomputing, sensors, big data, and powerful new software tools—collectively called *predictive analytics*—are dramatically improving product development.

In this chapter I will show how predictive analytics is helping researchers solve health sciences' biggest problems. I will also show how companies are using it to speed up development

83

time for new products and services—in the process, creating new business models. And I will explore how three dot-com era companies merged data and software to forge transformative predictive businesses in this growing field.

Speed Solves Everything

At face value, predictive analytics is not terribly complex. It's software that helps engineers quickly make better forecasts about the future.

The idea is to apply data mining, statistical modeling, and machine learning to large sets of historical and current data. Think of machine learning as a set of computer systems that become educated autonomously by processing data continuously. It's large-scale, rapid pace trial-and-error simulation.

Done right, it means the effective end of hit or miss in project development, management, and resource planning. It completely revamps the way products are discovered and optimized.

In its 2016–2017 IT Annual Performance report, **Intel** (INTC) credited predictive analysis for $653 million in annual savings across its sales, supply chain, factory, and manufacturing operations. The company was able to cut the time to market for new products by 39 weeks.

That kind of success does not go unnoticed. Data-driven decision making is one of the fastest growing trends in corporate boardrooms.

Bank of America (BAC) used predictive analytics to build a state-of-the-art chatbot called Erica. The software is equipped with artificial intelligence and cognitive messaging and lives inside a secure mobile app on a customer's smartphone. She knows all the intimate details of your finances. She is always learning, and you can chat with her through text or voice, just like a human assistant. Erica may suggest moving money to save you from bouncing a check. Or she may recommend a way to help you to save for a rainy day. She can even help improve your credit score.

The bank hopes bots are the answer to improving customer loyalty and systemwide productivity. Erica is one manifestation, and she's slick.

However, the use cases for predictive analytics far exceed bots and cost savings. The sudden ability to find patterns in large data sets and derive actionable insights is game changing. Right now, researchers in every sector are working with these tools. And they are making amazing discoveries.

Remaking IBM

Ginni Rometty, chief executive officer at **IBM**, likes to say that companies that fail to embrace cognitive computing—a mixture of big data, artificial intelligence, and predictive analytics—will be disrupted. It is a powerful message. The barriers to entry are lower than ever, and start-ups with new ways of thinking have changed the landscape.

That is certainly true at IBM. The one-time enterprise computing leader is a shadow of its former self, disrupted by Amazon.com, Alphabet, Salesforce.com, and a host of other agile companies that saw the potential of the cloud early.

Still, her point is well taken. Data, and predictive analytics in particular, have radically changed the way businesses operate and make decisions. "Many more decisions will be based on predictive elements versus gut instincts," Rometty told the corporate attendees at the Council on Foreign Relations in March 2013. She went on to emphasize that all businesses, whether they like it or not, will need to become data driven to compete. If they chose to ignore data analytics, they will not survive.

So far, they seem to be heeding her warning. IDC forecasts that big data and predictive analytics will grow from $130 billion annual spending in 2018 to $203 billion by 2020. The bulk of the growth will be concentrated in software, as reporting and analysis tools take center stage.

However, convergence with artificial intelligence means there will be room for growth for traditional hardware companies, too.

At the Strata + Hadoop conference, held in New York, September 2016, Martin Hall, chief data scientist for big data solutions at Intel, made that case succinctly: "We now have the data, the analytics, and the compute power to deliver more than insights—we can enable intelligence."

IBM has had some predictive analytics success stories. However, I'm not recommending IBM to investors. Its transformation is too little, too late.

T-Mobile, the giant US-based telecommunications firm, used data analytics to provide real-time, actionable insights to make significant improvements in its network.

Seton Healthcare, based in Austin, Texas, was able to reduce the number of patients being readmitted to hospital for congestive heart failure through the analysis of large amounts of unstructured data such as doctor notes, discharge summaries, and echocardiogram reports.

Analysis of streaming, real-time data is happening. Large enterprises are embracing it. And they are more willing than ever to look to software specialists. Many of these companies grew up in the dot-com era. They have learned how to use all of the tools that came from that era.

Investors should understand the growth story of predictive analytics is in the early phase. Companies that understand predictive analytics are going to be big winners.

Need a New Liver? Take a Number

Within a decade, people in need of a new liver, heart, or kidney will get a new one practically on demand. These brand-new organs will be regenerated from their very own cells.

That's according to one maverick expert, Dean Kamen. He is a serial inventor of medical devices, with 440 patents to his credit. That includes an electronic wheelchair that can climb and descend stairs, a robotic prosthetic arm, and the first portable insulin-delivery system.

Kamen believes regenerative medicine is the next big thing. And he says medical research is close to creating relatively inexpensive, engineered human organs.

Because these organs use the donor's own cells, their bodies would be far less likely to reject them.

It is the kind of emergent technology promised by science fiction.

Dr. McCoy on "Star Trek" points some gizmo at Captain Kirk, and all of his injuries magically disappear. Now, rapid advances in computing power, predictive analytics, and biotechnology are helping researchers make that USS Enterprise cinematic magic a reality.

The science starts by taking ordinary cells from blood or

the skin. Then those are converted to induced pluripotent stem cells. These cells are later transformed into the specific cells required to regenerate tissue.

BlueRock Therapeutics, a Boston-based start-up, raised $225 million in 2016 from Bayer and Versant Ventures. It focuses on allogeneic cells because they are the easiest to produce. They also don't have to come from the patient.

BlueRock hopes to regenerate tissue by developing stem cells that transform into cells that otherwise would not grow back.

For example, heart attack sufferers typically lose hundreds of millions of cells. Those cells are replaced by the body with rigid scar tissue.

In some cases, the lack of elasticity incapacitates the heart. The only remedy is a transplant.

BlueRock's strategy is to inject engineered heart muscle cells into the heart. In theory, the cells should regenerate new, healthy heart tissue. The plan is to do the same with brain cells to help patients suffering from Parkinson's disease.

It's not substantially different than the current wave of cellular therapies finding success in cancer research.

CAR T-Cell therapies use re-engineered cells to treat blood cancers. **Novartis** (NVS) showed the treatment eliminated an aggressive blood cancer (advanced lymphoblastic leukemia) in 82 percent of patients in clinical trials.

In many ways, Kamen's plans are more far-reaching. Called a modern-day Thomas Edison by *Popular Science*, he raised $300 million from venture capitalists and the federal government to change what is possible in medicine.

Kamen is heading the Advanced Regenerative Manufacturing Institute (ARMI) in Manchester, New Hampshire. He hopes to recruit two Big Pharma companies and a cottage industry of academics, universities, and smaller companies to work together on cutting-edge developments.

Already, he says a couple of researchers are on the cusp of mass-producing human blood.

Apart from eliminating the need for blood drives, it's also a key building block. Kamen sees collaborative groups using the science to regenerate skin, retinas, and eventually internal organs like livers, hearts, and kidneys.

It's the sort of vision that led the Department of Defense to kick in $80 million for ARMI.

None of this would be possible without predictive analytics. Kamen and his team are using software modeling and massive data sets to predict medical outcomes in a way that seems like science fiction. It's also the type of outcome investors need to get ahead of because it's coming, and it's going to be big. Maybe even revolutionary.

Building Life from Scratch

George Church, a noted Harvard geneticist, is one step closer to building synthetic human DNA.

Stat News reports that he met in mid-2017 with 130 scientists, lawyers, and government officials to discuss how development might proceed. Ethical issues aside, think about that for a moment. Church is not talking about just editing the building blocks of human life. He wants to re-create them in a lab.

And it is more feasible and more far-reaching than most laypeople think.

Church is no stranger to controversy. In his 2012 book,

Regenesis: How Synthetic Biology Will Reinvent Nature and Ourselves, he wrote about how humans with lab-made genomes might become immune to all viruses. According to Church, the process could be accomplished by simply removing the gene material that viruses need to replicate.

He also wants to reanimate the woolly mammoth and alter pig genes so their organs can be transplanted into humans.

In theory, resurrecting the prehistoric beast is now possible because scientists found perfectly preserved DNA material. And Church believes he can use CRISPR-Cas9, a gene-editing tool he helped develop, to work out the kinks of pig-to-human organ transplantation.

What is so fascinating, and game changing, is that synthetic human DNA makes even gene editing obsolete. Forget snipping. Scientists could simply build the exact genomes they want from scratch.

To get there, they will have to build on the pioneering work of Craig Venter, who was introduced earlier. In 2010, the geneticist led a team that created the first synthetic bacteria cell. What Church plans is exponentially larger and more complex.

Writing DNA is tedious and expensive work. It involves precisely manipulating tiny amounts of chemicals and a DNA molecule. These chemicals are the sugar-based building blocks designated A, T, C, and G. They must be added in the correct amounts and the proper order hundreds of times to change the structure of DNA.

However, the potential reward is huge. Apart from giving scientists a better understanding of genetic code, it should provide insight into the complexity of gene relationships.

That is where the possibilities begin. Immunities, designer babies, and reversing the aging process are definitely on the table. Better start shorting hospital and funeral services stocks.

The original project to read the human genome took 13 years and cost US taxpayers $3 billion. Church believes writing the human genome might cost $1 billion and take only ten years. That estimate may prove overly pessimistic.

Powerful public-cloud networks grow stronger every day. However, predictive analytics software is the key. Investors need to understand that all of the complex math and modeling is happening inside bespoke software. This code is finding patterns where none seem to exist, and it is in a constant state of refinement.

Gene editing is a powerful new tool for scientists, but discovery is being driven by software.

Netflix Knows What You Want to Watch

In 1997, a tiny Scotts Valley, California, company came up with a radical business model. The big idea was to use data to change the way people consume media.

That company was **Netflix** (NFLX). Founders Reed Hastings and Marc Randolph started with a humble DVD rent-by-mail website. It took off. However, growth caused a dilemma: Everyone wanted the new releases, but that would strain resources. The fix was an algorithm based on members' interests that de-emphasized popular titles.

By 2006, new releases represented less than 30 percent of Netflix's new rentals.

That's the power of our new age. Data analytics and predictive modeling empower entrepreneurs to build new business models with greater certainty. They deftly navigate traditional bottlenecks as competitors become stuck.

Jonathan Cohen, principal brand analyst at Amobee, a

global technology marketing firm, points out that Netflix's success stems largely from "using analytics to understand audiences" better than less savvy competitors. And as the company made the transition from rentals to streaming media, it pressed those advantages.

When I'm stretched out on the sofa, scanning my Netflix queue, ecosystems are the furthest thing from my mind. But Netflix knows what summaries I'm reading, how long I spend surfing titles, what I ultimately watch, and for how long. It's using all of that network data to keep me engaged and enhance my experience.

It's also using that data to predict, develop, license, and market new content. That's where Ted Sarandos comes in. He's the chief content officer. He knows network data is invaluable because it allows Netflix to build a business model around narrow casting, a personalized experience for each of its subscribers. It doesn't need blockbusters like ad-dependent networks.

That creates a lot of leeway.

Even when it spent $100 million for 26 episodes of "House of Cards," Netflix knew the deck was stacked in its favor. The political drama could be marketed to fans of the original British show. It could also be sold to the network's built-in fan bases for director David Fincher and actor Kevin Spacey (before he was dumped due to allegations of sexual improprieties).

Netflix understood what its viewers wanted before they knew.

It's an unconventional calculus that Sarandos used to build a wildly successful content portfolio. In March 2017 he extended the network's four-picture deal with "Saturday Night Live" alumni Adam Sandler because data showed that audiences loved Sandler films even if the critics hated them.

From the time of the original "House of Cards" content deal in 2013 to April 2018, there was a roughly threefold increase in Netflix subscribers; and, as a result, revenues increased from $4.37 billion to $11.69 billion through calendar 2017.

Netflix's algorithmic recommendations and personalized queue are now widely copied. In 2017, the company became the standard procedure for doing digital media distribution.

This is an exciting time for investors. So much is possible. Makers are not bound by old business models. Data analytics allows them to dream up new ones.

"We could see that eventually AMC was going to be able to do its own on-demand streaming," Hastings told the *New York Times* in June 2016. "We knew there was no long-term business in being a rerun company, just as we knew there was no long-term business in being a DVD-rental company."

The power of predictive analytics is very real.

HOW TO PLAY: Netflix shares have performed exceptionally well. Shareholders have seen average annual price increases of 50 percent since the beginning of 2007. It is hard to argue with that kind of success. Despite the stellar record of management, Netflix shares can be volatile. Plenty of traders routinely bet against the company. The odds are they are wrong. It's buyable on every important pullback.

Salesforce.com Has Customers' Number

Salesforce.com (CRM) was born in the throes of the Internet frenzy, 1999. To this day, it maintains the earmark of that era, a dot-com designation in its name.

Like most young companies of the era, the founders were

determined to radically change the way large enterprises interacted with customers. They felt customer relationship management could be systematic, more predictable.

The basic premise has not changed. Salesforce.com is still trying to improve relationships.

And if cofounder Marc Benioff has his way, artificial intelligence and predictive software will soon infuse every facet of the corporate world, making employees faster, smarter, and more productive.

While that might seem optimistic, Benioff has a history of getting enterprise productivity software right. Salesforce customer relationship management software has already had a huge impact on the way corporations interact with existing and prospective clients. What he hopes to do now is take that to the next level.

It seems to be working. The company posted fiscal 2018 revenues of $10.48 billion, a 25 percent increase over the previous year. Net income was $127.48 billion.

Recently Benioff has been investing heavily, buying smaller companies and hiring talent to build an artificially intelligent platform called Einstein. It's a big deal.

Einstein will not just consume and manage information like traditional CRM software suites. It will learn from the data. Ultimately it will understand what customers want before even they know. That would be a game changer in the CRM industry.

Building Einstein has not been easy or cheap. Salesforce started buying productivity and machine learning start-ups RelateIQ, MetaMind, and Tempo AI in 2014. In 2016, it acquired e-commerce developer Demandware for $2.8 billion; Quip for $750 million; Beyondcore for $110 million; three very small companies, Implisit Insights, Coolan, and PredictionIO for $58 million; and Your SL, a German digital consulting concern, to round out its German software unit. If all of that seems like a lot, it is. It's also $4 billion spent and, more important, a significant increase in head count.

During his quarterly conference call in September 2016, Benioff explained the rush: "We have been able to stitch all this together into this incredible AI platform, and this focus on AI and on the critical aspects of AI as the next wave of our industry has resulted in a machine-learning team of more than 175 data scientists who have built this amazing Einstein platform."

An integrated platform is the key to growth. Now with $10 billion in sales, Salesforce is aiming much higher. Parker Harris is the chief technology officer and cofounder of Salesforce. He has a strategy to push sales to $60 billion by 2034. Given his track record, investors should get on board.

Einstein will not just consume and manage information like traditional CRM software suites. It will learn from the data. Ultimately it will understand what customers want before even they know. That would be a game changer in the CRM industry.

The company expects to have new Einstein-enabled products—Sales Cloud, Services Cloud, Marketing Cloud, and Analytics Cloud—ready for developers during calendar 2018. They will be able to build applications on top of the clouds using their own code or Einstein extensions.

Grand View Research, a boutique San Francisco consulting firm, expects the CRM market to reach $81.9 billion by 2025. This is starting from a base of $26.3 million in 2015. The implied growth rate is 12 percent.

Salesforce dominates the CRM market. It is the biggest company in terms of revenues. It has the largest market share. And it is growing twice as fast at the implied growth rate from the Grand View Research note.

> **HOW TO PLAY:** Salesforce.com has been one of my
> long-term favorites. Shares have gained an average of
> 23 percent over a 10-year period beginning 2007. It is a
> stock that can be bought into weakness.

Focused on Future of Connections: PTC Inc.

PTC Inc. (PTC), which makes predictive analytics software tools, has been on a roll since 2009, and swept to new highs repeatedly in 2016, 2017, and 2018. And that is the least interesting part of the story.

The Massachusetts company sported a market capitalization of just $8.5 billion by early 2018, yet it consistently beat behemoths like **Oracle** (ORCL) and Siemens in job bids.

The secret is vision, planning, and execution.

Long ago, PTC bet its future on the promise of networks of connected things. Today, we call this the Internet of Things (IoT).

Back then, circa 1998, PTC software engineers began building Internet-based tools for Product Lifecycle Management, the idea that products should be designed to take into account inception, engineering design, manufacturing, service, and ultimately, disposal. At the time, it was a radical idea.

By 1999, PTC had 25,000 customers, including major brands in aerospace, automotive, industrial equipment, consumer products, high tech, and retail.

Today, Internet-based software suites are more the rule than the exception. PTC has three core businesses: Internet of Things, Computer Automated Design, and Product Lifecycle Management.

The last category is key. PTC is making predictive tools that have been especially useful to companies as they meticulously navigate through every stage of product development. By picking through massive amounts of historical data, informed with pattern insights, they are able to make more informed choices.

In 2017, PTC announced a major contact win from BMW. The German luxury carmaker planned to use a pair of PTC platforms to improve efficiency. Windchill, its PLM software suite, takes the guesswork out of real-world execution. And ThingWorx, a comprehensive industrial Internet of Things tool, should help BMW get data under control, and products to market faster and cheaper.

Faster, cheaper, and with fewer mistakes is hard to beat.

In January 2017, PTC was the surprise winner of a big contract from the US Air Force. The Pentagon was looking for a way to modernize the USAF supply chain. The deal covers 5,000 aircraft, 650,000 unique items, and 1,500 locations.

It didn't hurt that PTC's service parts management software was already in use at the US Navy, Coast Guard, **Boeing** (BA) and **Lockheed Martin** (LMT). According to the Pentagon, service levels at the Coast Guard improved 91 percent while operating costs have declined.

Writing for the *Harvard Business Review* in November 2014, James Heppelmann, PTC's chief executive, explained that connecting networks of things is the tip of the spear. Ultimately, the objective is to make machines smart, then completely transform competition.

It's a really big idea with potentially huge rewards.

McKinsey & Co., a research and consulting firm, predicts the IoT will have a $3.7 trillion impact on manufacturing alone by 2025.

There are other applications, too.

In February 2017, PTC announced a new partnership with the global consulting firm Deloitte to promote ThingWorx. The project is not far off Heppelmann's 2014 *Harvard Business Review* brief. ThingWorx software is a complete platform that allows developers to build software applications that interact in real time with sensors, utilities, and data analytics.

ThingWorx Analytics, for example, can detect anomalies and patterns in real-time data by using simulation and predictive analytics.

Vodafone is experimenting with smart cities. Its engineers are using ThingWorx and Vodafone's 5G networks, a next-generation wireless standard that could be up to 100 times faster than 4G, to enhance public transportation, reduce traffic congestion, and keep citizens safe. Buses, trains, and taxicabs become mere nodes on the network. Because the project is scalable, in the future the same solution will provide smart lighting, parking, and environmental monitoring.

HOW TO PLAY: Integration is the key competitive advantage PTC has over its competitors. It has a full suite of well-regarded software products. The stock market recognized the potential. Since 2007, shares have averaged 17 percent annually returns.

I have recommended PTC for years because I believe its managers have the vision and the commitment to make the company a big player in predictive analytics. Given the potential size of this market, even at a $9.0 billion valuation, the stock still looks cheap.

Fast Forward

Preconceived notions come easy. Conditioning has taught us to believe the most important breakthroughs occur in laboratories. We imagine scientists carefully pouring liquids into beakers and test tubes. Today, the most interesting developments in health sciences are coming from predictive analytic software models. Researchers are using these tools to discover relationships between compounds where none were thought to exist. And they are changing medicine in profound new ways. Dean Kamen's models predicted that regenerating human organs is possible. And work in the laboratory is bearing fruit.

It's all kind of surreal, but it is the product of pairing massive amounts of data with predictive analytic software, then running the code on supercomputers.

The best way to play the rise of predictive analytics is with the companies that pioneered the field in the dot-com era. PTC engineers have been toiling away since the early 1990s. Salesforce used predictive analytics to remake enterprise customer relationship management. And Netflix became the world's network by understanding how to engineer content its customers wanted. These are all great businesses with significant long-term growth potential even though they are already large companies.

CHAPTER 6

ARTIFICIAL INTELLIGENCE: COMPUTING EVOLVES

The human brain is a marvelous central processing unit. Even as babies, without life experiences, we learn quickly and efficiently. In contrast, computers have historically learned only through brute force and repetition. Sure, they can be programmed to do wonderful things. But to really learn and adapt, they require an amazing amount of raw processing power.

As the cost of processing power has plunged, scientists have finally discovered how to write and implement artificial intelligence routines that teach computers to learn how to solve problems using human-like logic. And successes have been impressive.

In this chapter I will delve into what is possible as computers begin to learn to think like humans. I will show how advances in sheer computing power, coupled with AI, mean that solutions to many of our biggest problems as a society are within reach—and conversely, why AI may create a batch of new problems. Then I will make the investment case for two companies that have established clear leads in this important new field.

AI: In the Beginning

For several decades, artificial intelligence was a pipe dream left to academics. The very idea that computers could learn the same way humans do seemed outside the realm of possibility. Computers lacked raw processing power and sufficient data sets to test the validity of their theories.

The cloud, sensors, and big data revived AI from the land of sci-fi. Now it is everywhere.

AI is actually not one thing. It is a broad range of computer science disciplines focused on helping computers learn independently. Because computers can process vast amounts of data quickly, they are very good at certain tasks like pattern recognition. This mode of AI is typically called *machine learning*.

Humans are able to process many different things at once. We can drive a car because we simultaneously acquire and process information through our eyes and ears, while understanding what that information means and how it changes over time. Raindrops or bugs are distinctly different from stones and birds. Our eyes adapt effortlessly from the bright sunshine of a mountain road to the sudden darkness of a tunnel.

Before enhancements provided by AI, computers could only perform a compound task when distinctly programmed with a set of specific binary, or yes/no, instructions.

AI simulates human logic by processing multiple information feeds in parallel using neural networks, which are special algorithms inspired by human biology. They mimic the way our brains and central nervous system process information and learn.

AI is far from perfect, but the science is improving dramatically. Powerful computers help AI neural networks run countless simulations, untethered to human frailty, to escape the bounds of linear thinking.

Google developed a set of AI neural networks to translate languages. In one case, the networks were taught to translate between Polish and Korean. After much trial and error, the nets developed their own language based on common pairs. Then the networks on their own solved the tricky translation problem, and they did it with increasing speed and accuracy.

Initially, engineers were perplexed. They could not determine how the networks accomplished this feat. Later, they concluded the AI had devised a brand-new language, or *interlingua*, to make sense of language pairs. Once it had the cipher, the rest was a snap.

Now teams of engineers at companies all over the world are delving into all facets of the field: Computer vision, machine learning, image recognition or deep learning, and speech recognition AI are making great strides.

For investors, the opportunities are endless. Software engineers are on the cusp of solving some of the biggest problems in science—and potentially creating new ones.

AI at War: Meet the "Slaughterbots"

Imagine swarms of tiny drones. Now, imagine them armed with lethal weapons and AI: tiny, flying killers.

It seems like bad science fiction. It's not.

The technology already exists, reports Alvin Wilby, an executive at Thales UK, a major European defense contractor.

In November 2017, Wilby told the Lords Artificial Intelligence Committee, a British government panel, that it's just a matter of time before terrorists unleash "swarms" of small, lethal smart-drones.

And other people who should know are worried, too.

Like Noel Sharkey, emeritus professor of artificial intelligence and robotics at the University of Sheffield, who told the Lords Artificial Intelligence Committee that he fears untested, makeshift technology could end up in the hands of terrorists, like ISIS.

At a web conference in Portugal, in November 2017, the late Stephen Hawking, a renowned theoretical physicist, was even more downbeat. He warned that the development of full artificial intelligence could spell the end of human civilization.

Elon Musk, the tech visionary behind Tesla and SpaceX, was more succinct. He declared that AI is "our biggest existential threat."

It's easy to dismiss such worries. However, we live in an era when information technology is progressing at an exponential rate. **Amazon**, **Intel**, and **Qualcomm** have already demonstrated drones capable of autonomous navigation and targeting.

Scaling up the technology to swarms would not require "any inventive step," says Sharkey.

In October 2017, the US Air Force demonstrated how a swarm of autonomous drones might be used for surveillance. Three F-18 Super Hornets released 103 drones with only a 12-inch wingspan. The diminutive Perdix devices shared a single software brain that was programmed with one purpose—to avoid radar installations. In the test, the drones behaved as one unit. There was no leader. As in nature, the swarm adapted to lost members.

The Pentagon started working on Perdix in 2011. The idea for small, swarming drones came from a group of aeronautics students at MIT. In September 2014, the project had its first test flight at the Edwards Air Force Base. A year later, 90 Perdix drones were tested for military surveillance in Alaska. And in October 2016, an F/A-18 Super Hornet dropped a swarm of Perdix drones over a test field at China Lake, California.

Larger weaponized drones with AI brains had become a mainstay in modern warfare.

In May 2016, the US Navy showed off a drone system that is launched into the sky like a missile.

Once airborne, Locust drones, loaded with microexplosives, form packs. Then the group communicates via custom radar. Collectively, they locate targets, then dive bomb, kamikaze-style.

Slaughterbots is a short film that melds the advances made by the military and private business into a single dystopian nightmare. The film's hook: "Watch what happens when the weapons make the decisions."

It's as scary as it seems.

However, all of the technology to make it happen exists today, and it is progressing at a rapid rate. Smartphones gave us micro-electro-mechanical systems (MEMs). Electric components, like accelerometers, GPS, and solid-state compasses, are finally small and inexpensive enough.

And because billions of people are carrying smart devices everywhere, there is enough data to finally fuel the AI revolution scientists promised decades ago. Algorithms are getting better every minute as they chew up and digest the deluge of data.

Along the way, investors have accumulated massive profits. With careful selection, the next step might be even more lucrative.

Artificial intelligence is creating distinct winners and losers. It is concentrating power among those firms that bet early and wisely. They have economies of scale. They also have the power to erect unique barriers to entry.

Hopefully, the drones of *Slaughterbots* will remain fiction. But their very possibility creates a bonanza for a few defense contractors that are focused on aircraft and missiles, like **Northrop Grumman** (NOC), **Raytheon** (RTN), and **Lockheed Martin** (LMT). Well-placed fears mean AI is likely to be a major new force magnifier in the industry.

The number of conglomerates capable of meeting this challenge is tiny.

Those companies, and their supplier ecosystems, are going to win an enormous prize when contracts get doled out in the heat of the paranoia.

Remember, these are government contracts. Companies need to meet stringent security guidelines.

I have been recommending defense contractors with major AI programs for years. This is a really big trend. It is going to happen, and investors need to begin taking positions now.

The genies are out of the bottle. And they've got self-guided bazookas over their shoulders.

Watch Your Back—Here Comes Ubiquitous Surveillance

Don't look now, but video surveillance is right behind you. It was inevitable. The willing surrender of privacy, the fear of bad actors, and the advent of advanced AI make a potent combination.

In mid-2017, police in Dubai began testing a diminutive self-driving car on city streets. The robotic rig, about the size of a baby buggy, features cutting-edge video gear, networked facial-recognition software, and an aerial drone in case undesirables go off-road.

Boosted by AI, video surveillance has become a service. And it is about to explode.

According to Markets and Markets, a global research consulting group, the appetite for Video Surveillance-as-a-Service (VSaaS) will grow from $30.37 billion in 2016 to $75.64 billion in 2022, a compound annual growth rate of 15.6 percent.

VSaaS providers and their component suppliers are poised to clean up.

Demand is surging thanks to the perception of rising crime rates, increased terror attacks, and the numb acceptance of video surveillance. Meanwhile, the cost of camera sensors, network storage, and computing power is plummeting.

Then there is automation. Video surveillance used to be labor intensive. Humans monitored video screens 24/7, though they sometimes nod off. They are being largely replaced by AI algorithms capable of recognizing faces and detecting movement, even in the dark.

And what public cameras don't capture, state-owned bots crawling pervasive social media do.

In Dubai, initial ambitions are much lower. *Wired* reported the emirate contracted with New Zealand's Martin Aircraft Co. to equip firefighters with jetpacks. This policing robot gambit seems to fit with the surveillance AI narrative. It's cool tech for a city or state that wants to be on the cutting edge.

The machines are being built by OTSAW Digital, a Singapore company. In a press release, its chairman, Ling Ting Ming, explained the goal is more about using robots to augment policing, rather than to track humans.

"Robots exist to improve the quality of human lives," Ling says.

Happy talk aside, I'm optimistic because new technologies normally lead to important new industries and to new business models, like VSaaS.

Despite the enormous potential market, the rise of VSaaS is something barely on investors' radar. While video surveillance in North America will not reach Chinese penetration any time soon, casual observation at airports or crowded public places like stadiums shows that the number of cameras is growing.

In the current environment of terror and travel bans, this development will grow dramatically.

However, navigating is important. Video surveillance hardware is a fragmented marketplace. The market for VSaaS software is even more complicated.

HOW TO PLAY: One possible pure play is the video compression and semiconductor firm **Ambarella** (AMBA), based in Silicon Valley. Through mid-2018 its shares were down 60 percent from their 2015 high but stabilized around the $40 area. It could easily make another stab at $70 or higher, as drone and security IP camera companies seek its chips' video processing capabilities.

Insurance Is Next in Line for AI Disruption

A tiny Chicago start-up is having a huge impact on insurance.

Lemonade Insurance Co. wanted to disrupt the way insurance companies do business. So it replaced brokers and paperwork with bots, machine learning, artificial intelligence, and a simple smartphone app.

Then the magic happened.

Policies are created in 90 seconds. Most claim payouts take just three minutes. The industry noticed. Now business models are changing everywhere.

It was really just a matter of time before a sea change arrived. Insurance has not changed materially since 13,000 homes were lost in the Great Fire of London in 1666. This change is coming at the hands of two serial entrepreneurs bent on doing social good.

If the horn-rimmed glasses, gray T-shirt, and jeans are not a giveaway, CEO Daniel Schreiber is on the idealistic side of entrepreneurship. Lemonade sells low-cost rental and household insurance on monthly subscriptions. It scrapes a small fee and stows the rest in case claims arise.

In most years, says Schreiber, there will be money left over. That excess is then donated to the charity of the policyholder's choice at the end of the year. Lemonade calls this process Giveback. The idea is to use money that would otherwise be profits for social good.

Also, in theory, removing the profit motive eliminates the inherent conflict of interest that insurers face when negotiating claim payouts.

It also gently discourages policyholders from embellishing claims.

None of this would be possible without cutting-edge technology. Lemonade is built on a foundation of artificially intelligent bots and a lot of machine learning cranking away in the background.

Software determines everything. What the policy should cost. What the payout should be.

Lemonade calls the results *instant everything*: coverage in seconds and claim payouts in minutes. Lemonade once settled a claim for a stolen Canada Goose jacket in only three seconds.

That is causing havoc in the industry. Time is money.

So stodgy insurance companies are stepping up their own technology game. Many are using customer-generated photos. Others are using AI-enhanced drones to survey claims that would otherwise require a special adjuster.

Liberty Mutual routinely sends operators with drones to survey damaged roofs. The devices save time and the expense and danger of sending someone up a ladder. The *Wall Street Journal* reports 40 percent of American auto insurers no longer use human adjusters in many cases.

Lemonade software asks policyholders to snap a photo and, in some cases, record video testimony of the damage and the incident. From there, it runs 18 separate anti-fraud algorithms to apply artificial intelligence to the hunt for deception.

Most cases are settled without human input. It's possible because smartphones are equipped with great cameras that transmit metadata by default.

Claims processed by AI algorithms can take two to three days at the longest. Those handled by humans usually take 10 to 15 days.

That means a significant savings that could stretch into billions of dollars. S&P Global Market Intelligence says investigating claims accounts for 11 percent of every dollar of premium collected.

There is also the problem of leakage. That is the difference between what insurers ultimately shell out and what the claim should have cost. A 2010 Booz Allen study showed costs increase directly with the life of an open claim.

And every dollar lost negatively impacts the bottom line.

The opportunity for investors is huge. Insurance companies that adapt quickly will see dramatic cost savings and fatter profits. New actuarial models are certain to evolve. Business models and corporate structures will follow.

Zendrive makes a smartphone app that uses machine learning algorithms and pattern analysis to make actionable safety insights both for individual vehicle owners and corporate vehicle fleet managers. It works by collecting data using the sensors in a smartphone. The algorithms understand if the driver is speeding, driving aggressively, has become distracted, or is using the phone. It then provides real-time analytics that is sent back to the insurer. Good drivers get lower rates.

Since the Silicon Valley company launched in 2013, it has logged more than 75 million miles of data. It has also attracted the likes of BMW as an investor, and General Re as an insurance partner.

And the barriers to entry are nothing more than a simple smartphone, something owned by around 90 percent of US adults.

Another firm, Cape Analytics, is using AI-enhanced computer vision to make accurate property assessments for insurers without the need to send out an adjuster.

The company operates on the premise that the best way to write a policy is to have accurate information from the beginning. Cape uses satellite imagery and machine learning to build a robust database of key attributes. When customers apply for insurance, the key data has already been collected, leading to faster approval times and lower costs.

And everything is stored in the cloud, based on real-time data.

HOW TO PLAY: One of the few public companies operating in this space is **Guidewire Software** (GWRE). The company makes software products for the insurance sector, and it has been a very steady grower. Sales surged from $300 million in 2013 to $514 million in 2017. Net income was up 41 percent in 2017 to $21.2 million. It's on the cutting edge of AI, insurance, and fraud detection.

Nvidia Bets Big on "Deep Learning"

From 2014 to 2017, shares of semiconductor maker **Nvidia** (NVDA) advanced 1,167 percent. While that gain is crazy, investors may still be underappreciating the scale of the opportunity of this premier AI firm going forward.

The essence of Nvidia, and its hold on the future of computing, is based on artificially intelligent software. That is a long way from where it began: designing cutting edge chips, the hardware brains in computers.

Long ago, the company committed to data science that helps computers to see, think, and learn like humans. Deep learning, a type of AI based on graphic processing units, has been embraced by computer scientists. That rapid adoption by cutting-edge customers is driving Nvidia's bottom line.

Humans make snap decisions based on experience. If we're traveling on a freeway and a bug is hurtling toward the windshield, well, it's a bad day to be a bug. Until recently, computers had to stop, process the threat posed by the bug, and then decide what action to take. It was complicated.

That's because conventional computer architecture is sequential. Deep learning is based on a new model where billions of software neurons and trillions of connections run in parallel, in networks.

In 2011, Alphabet's secretive Google Brain learned to identify cats and people by endlessly watching cat videos on YouTube. That seemingly simple feat required 2,000 central processing units and Google's vast data center network. Later, Stanford University managed to replicate this by using deep learning and just 12 Nvidia accelerated GPUs. By 2015, researchers at Google and **Microsoft** (MSFT) used deep learning AI to beat humans in image recognition.

"By collaborating with AI developers, we continued to improve our GPU designs, system architecture, compilers, and algorithms, and sped up training deep neural networks by 50x in just three years—a much faster pace than Moore's Law," wrote Jen-Hsun Huang, Nvidia's founder and chief executive.

Huang is comfortable with uncommon choices. Wearing a leather jacket at corporate functions and flashing tattoos, his company cut its teeth two decades ago making high-end graphics cards, the PC hardware that turns code into images.

But it's come a long way since then. Its clientele, mostly gamers, demanded photorealistic imagery. So, Huang pushed the company to invest heavily in developing better software modeling.

And then . . . it clicked. Nvidia was sitting on a completely new method of computing.

It used artificial intelligence to combine traditional instruction processing from CPUs with data processing from graphic processing units.

This result did not come cheap. The *New York Times* reports that Nvidia has spent $10 billion developing its GPU computing platform.

Given the initial size of the company, that was a huge bet.

The impact for deep learning has been enormous. Researchers in healthcare, life sciences, energy, financial services, manufacturing, entertainment, and automotive are innovating at a frenetic pace.

Tesla (TSLA) in 2017 showed a self-driving vehicle equipped with Nvidia Drive PX hardware. The car successfully navigated busy residential streets, winding country roads, and the interstate before parallel parking in front of the corporate storefront. Daimler, Audi, and others are using Nvidia neural networks to advance their self-driving platforms, too.

The Drive PX Pegasus, the latest AI computer from Nvidia, can process 320 trillion operations per second. That's enough horsepower to deal with cameras, LiDAR, ultrasound, and any other sensor data required for full autonomy. And it fits inside a container the size of a lunchbox.

It's no wonder taxi, trucking, and logistics companies are clamoring to get their hands on it.

Meanwhile, Nvidia is pushing forward with new products and new markets.

In December 2017, the company revealed the Titan V. It's a $3,000 graphics card powerhouse. Yet it is not meant for graphics. Its purpose is to extend Nvidia's GPU computing platform to the next generation of workstations.

Investors should take note of this kind of forward thinking. This is what great companies do.

Today, GPUs are standard fare in the field of AI. From university researchers to bitcoin miners, smart coders are using the platform to push the limits of learning. In the process, Nvidia has attempted to break free of the cyclical nature of the semiconductor business.

The company put itself in the business of solving big problems by using AI.

Fortune named Huang as its Businessperson of the Year for 2017. That's cool . . . but a decade late.

Gartner, the global IT consulting firm, predicts migration to the cloud is a $1 trillion opportunity by 2020. Public cloud companies Amazon Web Services, Microsoft Azure, Google Cloud, Baidu, Oracle, Alibaba, and Tencent are all investing heavily in AI.

They see it as a value-added service—a way to entice corporate customers. And they want to make sure they are covering all bases. So in addition to their own CPU-based AI frameworks, each enthusiastically supports Nvidia's GPU.

To put the momentum of its data center business in perspective, sales were $1.93 billion in fiscal 2018, up 3x in just three years.

Titan V brings the same components found in Nvidia's $10,000 data center compute cards to the desktop. This means 5,120 compute cores, 640 machine-learning cores, 21 billion transistors, and the Volta GPU architecture.

All of this adds up to a monumental performance leap over everything in the marketplace.

It will allow researchers and developers to build AI software models right at their desk. More important, it extends GPUs into more applications.

And that will help Nvidia sell more hardware. It is a virtuous circle.

I have been directing investors to buy Nvidia shares for

years. The attraction was not AI originally. Rather, it was smart management. And sure enough, the company leveraged its graphics expertise into an entirely new way to solve complex problems. When the advantage was apparent, it bet big.

This is the attribute investors should seek. Great companies are focused. They leverage talents. When it's clear they have a competitive advantage, they strike and chew up the competition.

HOW TO PLAY: Nvidia shares' massive advance are underpinned by solid fundamentals: In fiscal 2018, sales were $9.71 billion, up 2.8x from 2009, and all signs point to more upside ahead, as I believe the company will continue to find new applications for AI using GPUs. Nvidia shares are one of the best ways to invest in artificial intelligence at this time and are therefore a buy on any significant pullbacks.

Alphabet's Long Bet on AI

Long before Nvidia's moonshot, and two decades before the company changed its name to Alphabet, Google was the quintessential artificial intelligence company.

It revolutionized Internet search with machine learning way back in January 1994. It hired the brightest minds in the field. It even began fiddling with code for self-driving cars as early as 2009.

Aside from becoming one of the biggest Internet businesses on the planet, its prowess in the field of AI didn't really get a lot of attention. Then, in January 2014, the company acquired a British AI company called DeepMind Technologies.

Demis Hassabis, its charismatic founder, had been teaching computers how to play video games as well as humans. Using a set of custom algorithms, and a Neural Turing machine, an external computing device that mimics human short-term memory, he was making tremendous progress.

That caught the attention of the Google founders.

Now DeepMind says its newest neural networks no longer require human input.

This clandestine Alphabet unit has been at the vanguard of AI research for a while. But this latest development is ground-breaking.

And the implications for everything from drug discovery to materials design are huge.

At first glance, what DeepMind is doing might seem trivial. Its AI efforts have been largely restrained to what looks like highbrow parlor tricks. In May 2017, AlphaGo, its strategy game-playing neural networks, became the first AI program to beat a human Go player. And not just any player—Lee Sedol was an 18-time Go world champion.

Go is a Chinese board game for two players developed 2,500 years ago. It involves opposing stones placed on a 19x19 grid. The objective is to surround more territory than your opponent.

The AlphaGo victory made headlines. Go is infinitely more complex than chess. It also stretches the limits of human general intelligence. Previously, it was something researchers found difficult to replicate with machines.

AlphaGo was the product of months of human training and countless computational hours. When Sedol was defeated 4-to-1, it validated unproven AI theories. It meant current artificial general intelligence structures were far enough along to replicate high-level human intelligence.

And now, DeepMind's AlphaGo Zero takes this to another level. Researchers presented Zero with the game rules, a board, and game piece markers only. There were zero human trainers, zero strategy lessons.

The AI learned Go in 72 hours by playing against itself in 4.9 million simulations. To improve, it had to continuously rethink the algorithms it was generating.

Then researchers matched Zero with AlphaGo. It was ugly. Zero slaughtered AlphaGo, 100-to-0.

It accomplished this with one neural network, four processors, and no human helpers. It invented super-successful strategies that humans had never considered. By contrast, AlphaGo needed two networks, 48 processors, and months of human coaching.

Some smart people have made pointed observations about the need to govern the speed of AI development. Bill Gates, Elon Musk, Stephen Hawking, and others fear military applications. You can imagine the harm a weaponized AI machine might cause if its sole purpose was to kill humans. Now, imagine the same machine endlessly refining its skills at an exponential rate.

Dictators understand the military opportunity. Vladimir Putin, the president of Russia, recently said the country that dominates AI will be the leader of the world.

It's enough to give the Terminator goose bumps.

On the other hand, AI machines unencumbered by human limitations should be capable of astonishing feats. The ability to run endless simulations is only limited by computer power, and that is progressing exponentially. New, ultra-efficient AI chipsets are operational. Next-generation hardware is in development.

It's a brave new world. Almost anything is possible.

Nvidia has an entire division devoted to designing AI architectures for the pharmaceutical industry. Researchers are using deep learning to understand vast amounts of bioscience data. They are developing personalized medicine and attacking Parkinson's, Alzheimer's, and cancer.

DeepMind is using its networks to better understand quantum chemistry. It's early, but Hassabis dreams of finding a room-temperature superconductor that would revolutionize battery development.

Investors need to understand the landscape has changed. They need to be aware some sectors will be disrupted, while others will thrive.

New Google DeepMind Technology Has a Mind of Its Own

Alphabet is in a unique position. It is the premier artificial intelligence company in the world, hands down. Everything the company does revolves around AI, and the data it needs to feed hungry algorithms.

Larry Page, the cofounder of Alphabet, tells an interesting story about how the fledgling Google fell into Internet advertising. He and Sergey Brin, a brilliant computer scientist, were working in the same office at Stanford University. Page had an idea. In the spring of 1996, the Internet was blossoming and he thought mapping the link structure of Internet pages, and their relationship, might be an interesting endeavor.

In March 1996, Page launched BackRub, an army of search bots with the task of determining web page back-links. These spiders endlessly crawled the web, cataloging links based on citations. As the project became more complex, Brin was drawn in. He was the same age as Page, but two years ahead academically because he completed his undergrad degree at age 19.

The project grew. It became PageRank. Page and Brin worked tirelessly, developing new math to solve the emerging problems. Brin explained that PageRank basically made the entire Internet into a math equation with several hundred million variables. Unwittingly, Brin and Page had developed the best search engine available. What made it so was relevancy and its recursive underpinnings. It got better and better with more data—an AI virtuous circle.

In the late 1990s, the dot-com boom was in full bloom. Both Yahoo and Excite, another popular search engine at the time, were born at Stanford. Page and Brin tried to sell the PageRank technology to Excite for the modest sum of $1.6 million and Excite stock. The offer was rejected. Excite saw itself as a portal, a destination. It scoffed at the idea that search could be an important part of the business.

So Brin and Page decided to go it alone. Armed with $100,000 in seed capital from the founder of Sun Microsystems, himself a Stanford alumnus, the company became Google, a name taken from the intentional misspelling of googol, the number one followed by 1,000 zeros.

By 1999, Google was performing seven million searches per day. There was no promotion. No advertising budget. And initial plans to license its search technology to Internet portals and corporate websites met with limited success. In order to fund the growth of the business, and further machine learning, Brin and Page reluctantly developed an advertising business model.

At the time, advertising was the only way to exploit machine learning.

Ultimately, a licensing deal with Yahoo gave Google the data it needed to prefect its algorithm. Searches grew to 100 million per day.

By 2002, advertising on Google got an upgrade. In addition to paying per click and placement, advertisers got the opportunity to bid against competitors' ads. This introduced relevancy. It also meant advertisers might end up paying less per ad, as long as they were more relevant to the searcher, and clicks increased.

The redesign was an immediate hit. In the first year, the company did $440 million in sales and $100 million in profits. It was also a new source of important data.

That has been the business plan ever since. Alphabet fits businesses around its AI exploits. It started with Search. Then came YouTube and Gmail. When the iPhone arrived, executives immediately understood smartphones would become a data goldmine. In the spring of 2005, Google purchased Android, a competing smartphone platform being developed by Andy Rubin.

Rubin promised Android would have the flexibility of Linux and the global reach of Windows.

Through mid-2018, Android commanded 82 percent of worldwide market share and is a fountain of data for Alphabet engineers. And they have other irons in the fire as well.

The company is pushing the limits of AI with self-driving cars, biotechnology, home automation, and connectivity. For Alphabet, the attraction is data to feed its algorithms. The business purpose will come later. Sales growth in 2017 topped 23.7 percent, exceedingly fast for a company of its size.

Sales and profits are accelerating as the company leverages its dominant digital platforms into other parts of the economy with AI. For many, Alphabet is an advertising business. Judging by sales and success, it certainly appears that way. It is the dominant digital advertising platform in the world. This misses the point. Advertising is merely a tool. It is the application of machine learning.

Alphabet has designs on changing the entire world by understanding the relationships between data and real-world events. And the company has more data and more engineers than any other business.

HOW TO PLAY: Alphabet shares are a good, well-rounded way to play AI; buy on pullbacks.

Fast Forward

For a lot of us, AI is terrifying. We routinely dismiss all of the amazing possibilities of computers learning to think like humans because we are deeply aware humans do a lot of self-destructive things. The prospect of armies of soulless computers learning all of our bad habits at hyper scale is apocalyptic.

It does not have to be that way. Certainly, there are military and surveillance applications. The world is still a dangerous place. It makes sense that those we trust to keep us safe will use every technological advance to ramp up the war against bad actors. However, many firms are now using AI to build self-driving vehicles, design safer infrastructure, and find treatments for diseases and genetic disorders. Solving these big problems will save countless human lives.

Commercial applications are endless, too. Open AI platforms and cloud computing will bring massive simulation and virtually unlimited supercomputer processing power to everyone with a good idea. Entrepreneurs will be able to build new products, services, and business models, and then test them endlessly in simulations until they get it right.

Nvidia and Alphabet are the two leading AI companies in the world. Both companies bet early and often that AI would be the most important technological advance of this generation. They won. In the process, their technologies have become foundational.

Nvidia's deep learning AI is being embraced as a standard at every data center in the world. This means insatiable demand for its hardware for the foreseeable future. Alphabet staked its claim in 1999 with BackRub. It has always been a machine-learning company first. All of its other businesses, including Internet advertising, have only been practical ways to advance AI research. There is every reason to believe managers will use the company lead to bring AI to media, real estate development, autonomy and health sciences, and all vibrant longer-term businesses.

CHAPTER 7

ROBOTICS: RISE OF THE MACHINES

Most of us have seen pictures of the inside of modern factories. Hordes of giant metal robots twisting and tilting are not a surprise. What might be surprising is how smart they are getting. Like most things, robots have been fast-forwarded with better sensors, vision, network capability, data analytics, and very often artificial intelligence.

In this chapter I will chronicle the rapid advancement of robotics from bipedal search and rescue units to cutting-edge biomechanical prosthetics. I will provide insight to where the industry is headed. And I will explore three little known firms with bright prospects that have become niche leaders.

It Starts with Software

It seems like once a week the *Guardian* or *Economist* runs a story about the coming robot apocalypse. Lately, even the *Wall Street Journal* has gotten into the act. So you know it's bad.

They're not talking about killer terminators and Skynet stuff. It's more along the lines of robots that are going to steal your job, ruin the economy, and make life a living hell for your grandkids.

The worry is that robots are getting smarter. I mean way smarter—and potentially capable of independent thought.

They can now see with low-cost, high-definition cameras. They can hear with ultrasonic sensors. They can touch and even feel with dexterous limbs. They can think, too. And all of this is getting better at an exponential rate.

In 2015, the DARPA Robotics Challenge put robotic development to the test. Following the Fukushima Daiichi nuclear calamity, the goal was to build a general-purpose robot capable of disaster relief in hazardous situations. With millions of dollars in prize money hanging in the balance, prototypes from several leading engineering schools and robotics start-ups raced through an obstacle course designed to test their rescue skills. The robots drove cars, cut holes in walls, and opened valves. They just couldn't seem to navigate stairs.

That was June 2015. You should see what they are capable of now.

It's a sign of the things to come.

Jerry Kaplan, in his 2015 book, *Humans Need Not Apply*, summed it up perfectly: "If you own the robots you're going to do great, so get ready to make a lot of money. Robots will accelerate income inequality. However, if your job is repetitive, you're in deep trouble."

I'm an optimist. I believe society will figure out a way to survive the socialization of robots. We adapt. The real opportunity is for investors.

This is the beginning of something really big.

Japanese life insurer Fukuko Mutual, in January 2017, said it will replace 34 insurance claim workers with robots powered by IBM Watson Explorer software that are capable of reading medical certificates and records and factoring the length of hospital stays, given a particular surgical procedure, before calculating likely payouts. Fukuko officials believe the cost savings will total more than $1 million per year after the initial outlay.

These robots are not Hollywood chic. They are not even tangible. They're just bits of code, 1s and 0s, structured to interpret data and reduce the cost of labor, in that order. Now they are ready to be deployed in large numbers.

No job is safe, according to researchers at Stanford University. Lawyers, accountants, and even surgeons can be automated away. Artificial intelligence is accelerating robots' education. They are already good at repetitive judgment tasks based on data analysis and are deployed throughout large companies in customer service, quality control, fraud analysis, diagnosis, and treatment systems. Every new data point makes them better and cheaper.

Fukuko spent just $1.7 million to install Watson, and the contract calls for an outlay of $128,000 per year on maintenance. Trading people for software will pay for itself in only two years. After that, all of the savings go straight to the bottom line. You can imagine how quickly financial officers are lining up for some AI robotics business magic.

And that's the kicker. Investing in robotics AI makes good business sense in this new age. Research firm IDC predicts demand for cognitive systems will grow at an incredible rate: from just $8 billion in 2016 to $47 billion by 2020. Industries now most targeted for robotics include banking, securities and investments, and manufacturing. A researcher noted that in these areas are found a "wealth of unstructured data, a desire to harness insights from this information, and an openness to innovative technologies."

These changes are not far off in the future. They're here right now. For much of the past 100 years, American wage growth had risen in lockstep with productivity but in 1990 the two began to diverge. There is a good reason for this. Work can be divided into four types: routine, nonroutine, manual, and cognitive. Routine is different than nonroutine because it does not vary. Manual is different than cognitive because it involves physicality.

In 1990, the St. Louis Federal Reserve Bank found that the growth of routine manual work, like that performed by conventional factory workers, began to slow because it was relatively easy for software engineers to write rules that robots could follow. More recently it has become easier to write rules for routine cognitive work, like that performed by millions of Americans working in offices.

We can see these changes in real time. When Amazon.com purchased the robotics firm Kiva in 2012, few observers expected the dramatic impact automation would have on its warehouse floors. In September 2017, the *New York Times* reported robot deployment at the online retailer had swollen to more than 100,000. Human workers in Amazon warehouses have been cut by two-thirds, and those who remain perform only non-routine tasks.

And then there is WhatsApp, the software messaging platform that Facebook purchased for $19 billion in 2014. That firm serves more than a billion users and sends 34 billion messages per day with just 55 employees and 32 software engineers.

In January 2016, the World Economic Forum estimated that as many as five million jobs could be lost to automation by 2020. That estimate assumes little progress in deep learning and other forms of artificial intelligence. Andrew Ng, chief scientist at **Baidu** (BIDU), figures that is way too optimistic. He warns artificial intelligence advances will "create massive labor displacement." And he is not alone in this assessment. The question is what political leaders will do about it.

Surgical Robotics Comes of Age

In August 2017, surgeons at the University of Pennsylvania medical school did something amazing.

Noah Pernikoff, a commercial contractor, developed a rare tumor where the base of his skull met his spine. Removal was dangerous. Any error could result in loss of primary senses, fine motor skills, and even total paralysis. And if surgeons failed to remove all of the tumor, it could grow back, perhaps more aggressively, putting the patient in more jeopardy. So the surgeons made a decision. They asked for help from **Intuitive Surgical** (ISRG), the company that developed the da Vinci robotic surgery system.

Since 2005, medical robots have benefitted enormously from advances in information technology. Intuitive Surgical has been at the vanguard of that advance. Its da Vinci Surgical System helps surgeons perform better by putting them in a better position. The doctors sit comfortably at a networked, virtual reality operating station. They see a three-dimensional representation of the actual operation. Using foot pedals to maneuver the camera, and special finger-operated master controllers, they manipulate real medical instruments attached to four robotic limbs. At the same time, da Vinci system processors are performing millions of internal safety tests, for enhanced surgical precision. Hand tremors are eliminated.

It seems like some mad scientist stuff, but it's cutting edge, literally.

Pernikoff's case is special because of the location of his cancer. Chordoma is a slow-growing cancer that occurs in the bones of the spine and skull. Worldwide, it affects only one million patients annually, and most cases can be treated with minimally invasive surgery. In the case of Pernikoff, the tumor impacted his C2 vertebrae, the part of the cervical spine that allows us to move our heads from side to side. C2 is also uniquely shaped, allowing the vertebral arteries to reach through to the brain and supply it with blood.

Surgery seemed out of the question. Then, Pernikoff was referred to the Hospital of the University of Pennsylvania. Researchers there had developed a minimally invasive transoral robotic surgery to remove tumors through the mouth and throat.

A team of experts, led by Dr. Neil Malhortra, an assistant professor of neurosurgery, and Dr. Bert W. O'Malley Jr., chairman of otorhinolaryngology, put together a three-part plan. First, surgeons made an incision at the back of the neck. They used ultrasonic tools to make a series of bone cuts, without impacting the tumor. Malhortra followed with the transrobotic surgery to remove the tumor. In the last stage, surgeons reconstructed the spinal column using bone from Pernikoff's hip.

The surgery was a two-day marathon, but it was also a stunning success.

It was also the first-ever use of a robot to remove a tumor in this location. Pernikoff returned to work as a commercial contractor for the city of New York. He was grateful that his cancer was caught in time, and that technological advances in robotics made surgery possible.

A Real "Bionic" Man

Remember the TV series, "Six Million Dollar Man"? Johns Hopkins and the Department of Defense have finally brought that idea to life.

It is not a complete reboot of the 1970s fantasy. Johnny Matheny, the recipient, is not an astronaut. He will not be able to run 60 mph.

But in December 2017 he got to take home a prototype $120 million bionic arm. It changed his life and will put a smile on your face.

It is also a wake-up call for investors. Robotics technology infused with advanced artificial intelligence is real and is proliferating in unexpected ways.

Johnny is not what you might expect. He doesn't have Hollywood good looks, nor does he cut an especially impressive figure. Goateed and balding, his midsection is impressive.

He is an ordinary West Virginia guy and a self-labeled hillbilly. But he is good-natured, and he claims to live his life by two enduring rules: "There is a reason for this season," and "always have positive mental attitude."

It would have been easy to give up. In 2005, doctors discovered a very aggressive cancer in his left forearm. "Six surgeries trying to cut it out," he quips, "and 39 radiation treatments trying to burn it out."

None of that worked. By 2008, his doctors had exhausted every treatment. Amputation was the only way to ensure the mutation did not spread.

Through all of it, Johnny forged onward.

While browsing on the Internet, he found a link to Modular Prosthetic Limb (MPL). That's a new artificial arm being jointly developed by Johns Hopkins Applied Physics in Maryland. He also landed at DARPA's site. That's the advanced research arm of the US Department of Defense.

The MPL has 26 joints. Seventeen of them can be moved independently. But the big innovation is mind control. Using a Bluetooth armband and a special implant fused directly to the bone, wearers can control the arm by simply thinking.

The process is complicated. Johnny had two surgeries. The first attached the implant to his bone. Then surgeons moved nerves in his upper arm nearer to the elbow. Johnny had to learn how to access the missing neural information from those nerves through a process called reinnervation. It was a long and tedious process that continues to this day.

When it all works, those nerves activate sensors in the Bluetooth armband that control the robotic arm.

Johnny was one of a handful of people selected to begin testing the device. Albert Chi, a trauma surgeon at Johns Hopkins, located the nerves in Johnny's arm that before had controlled his hand. Chi surgically moved the nerves to healthy tissue and fitted the osteointegrated implant.

Since September 2014, Johnny has been learning how to control the arm. His progress is amazing.

All of this has been accomplished on a part-time basis. The MPL is a $120 million device. Johnny traveled to Baltimore every three months to work with Chi and researchers in a controlled environment. They slide the device onto the implant, and Johnny's quadrupedal journey would resume.

That changed in Christmas 2017. He has been living with the device full-time, in his own home, in an experiment that will last all of 2018. He will be completely on his own, free to make mistakes and push the MPL to its natural limits. Researchers have asked that he not wear it while driving, and that he should keep it dry. But beyond that, he is free to do as he pleases, at least through 2018.

Johnny Matheny may not look like the $6 million man, but he represents the same hopes and aspirations. He has become the living embodiment of what robotic technology can do to make those who lose limbs feel whole again.

Granted, at $120 million, not everyone will get this opportunity. However, there are companies like **Mazor Robotics** (MZOR) that are making an impact right now. The Israeli company makes a surgical robot that is making tremendous progress with spinal cord surgeries. More on Mazor in a moment.

Investors need to get ready. This is a real investment story with plenty of upside.

You're Gonna Flip Over This Robot

Two years ago, the best bipedal robots couldn't climb stairs or open doors. Watching them calculate vertical distances, shake, and then tumble was hilarious.

Now, Boston Dynamics has one doing backflips.

In November 2017, the company showed off its latest iteration in the development of robots that walk like people. They call it Atlas.

After some software enhancements, Atlas now has an uncanny sense of balance. It can jump up on a stand, then hop to face the opposite direction. And, yes, Atlas can even perform backflips like a gymnast.

Scary, sure, if it evades control and has a mind of its own. But don't miss the bigger picture. This is an opportunity for investors.

We humans have been trained to fear robots, especially the ones that look like us. In books and movies, they have this pesky habit of blowing explorers and scientists to smithereens. In reality, they represent what is possible.

At the 2017 GPU Technology Conference—or as techs call it, "the GTC"—Jensen Huang, chief executive of semiconductor maker **Nvidia** (NVDA), explained how his company taught a software robot named Isaac to play hockey.

Huang's researchers first constructed a virtual, photorealistic alternative universe that obeyed the laws of physics. The virtual world had ice, pucks, hockey sticks, and even movable nets. The engineers added virtual sensors and let Isaac learn by trial and error.

Then they duplicated the robot hundreds of times and continued the simulation.

Because the universe was virtual, there was no limit to the number or the speed of the simulations. Isaac was continually refined and, very quickly, mastered the physics of hockey.

Huang believes the same massive-simulation learning program will have profound implications for healthcare. He sees robotic surgeons that will develop skills far superior to humans.

And the process has already yielded impressive results for self-driving cars. In October 2017, Huang told the *Times of*

Israel he expects fully autonomous taxis will be in operation as early as 2020.

These developments are impressive. They are also indicative of the amazing opportunities available to investors right now.

Utilitarian robotaxis will share the road with modified delivery vans and truck fleets. Tractors and earthmovers have been autonomous for a generation. Refinements in software will add value to those products.

Bots and blockchains, which you'll learn about in Chapter 8, will cut billions of dollars in regulation bloat and the head counts at forward-thinking banks, brokers, and insurers.

The advance of software robots is materially changing the business models for a number of companies. Many of the ramifications have not been fully reflected in the stock prices.

When bipedal robots struggled with simple tasks at the DARPA Robotics Challenge in 2015, critics could not contain their laughter. They looked at the collections of aluminum, copper wire, and sensors and surmised that a solution must involve a complete redesign.

They missed the story. It was a software challenge. The future of robots is smart.

The Robot Revolution Began with Patent 9,785,911

The latest phase of the robot revolution began October 10, 2017. The catalyst was US Patent No. 9,785,911.

This patent was being granted to Pittsburgh-area start-up IAM Robotics for its Swift Solution Suite's system and methods.

IAM also developed Swift, the world's first autonomous and mobile warehouse robot, which is designed to pick out products and put them where its owners want them to go.

Swift is a milestone for engineering and a touchstone for workers.

For investors, this could be the opportunity of a generation.

Industrial robots have become vital to manufacturing productivity. Giant mechanical arms spot weld, stamp metal, and help workers move heavy materials precisely into position. In warehouses, pint-sized robots zip across concrete floors, carrying heavy racks of parts to help workers complete customer orders.

Swift is an evolution. Workers are not required.

It is part of a suite that includes IAM Flash, a 3D item scanner, and SwiftLink, its fleet management software. Together, Swift can navigate unmodified settings, find items, and place them into bins.

Living up to its name, Swift performs these tasks twice as fast as humans.

It is already operational at a New York drug wholesaler. In 2014, a proof-of-concept robot, nicknamed Adam, began cruising the 19,000-square-foot warehouse at the Rochester Drug Cooperative. The system could scan and digitally re-price shelved items. It was operational within 24 hours.

Adam has evolved into Swift, a workhorse robot. It has a hot-swappable battery and the capability to work continuously for 10 hours at a pace impossible for humans.

The Swift robot can ID items, grab them with a suction arm, and either drop them in a processing bin or return them to a shelf—all faster than humans could ever dream of.

Speed is a big part of the robot revolution.

Jack Ma, chief executive of **Alibaba Group Holding Inc.** (BABA), China's biggest e-commerce company, told CNBC in June 2017 that automation will mean future workers might spend only 16 hours per week on the job. It will be a bonanza for the travel and hospitality industries, he predicts.

He also warned that getting there might be painful. Populism will rise, and governments will be under pressure to rework social safety nets, as the ranks of unemployed swell unimaginably.

IAM Robotics is a privately held company. But there are plenty of other ways to invest in the next industrial revolution that's already underway.

Yasakawa Electric Corp. (YASKY) began as a supplier of electric motors to the coal mining industry. Today, its industrial robots are dominant on factory floors all over the world with tasks like arc welding, painting, and assembling. More on Yasakawa in a moment.

Robotics is the cornerstone of Industry 4.0, a business buzzword that includes automation, cloud and cognitive computing, and the Internet of Things. And it is going to be huge.

Boston Consulting Group, a leading industry researcher expects this to be a multitrillion-dollar opportunity. Every facet of manufacturing must adapt. The consultants' Factory of the Future white paper forecasts these changes in great detail.

As the physical world becomes digital, every manufacturing and service process will transform. Future factory and warehouse floors will be about the collection of data. It will become the new currency for improving productivity.

Musk's Next Space Shot:
Factories Without Humans

Elon Musk is obsessed with improved productivity.

In September 2016, Musk, the founder and chief executive officer of **Tesla**, sent a letter to shareholders. He promised that next-generation robotic investments could speed up the production line by twenty times over in two years—to 20,000 vehicles per month.

By March 2018, production of the entry level Model 3 reached 2,000 per week. Including legacy Model S, and X models, the Freemont, California, plant was making 3,500 units every week.

Musk bet the life of his fledging electric car company on robots, and he was making headway.

Critics still argue it's not enough. Tesla is a controversial company, and Musk has become a P.T. Barnum–like character. Often, his wild promises go unfulfilled. Although the company is making production progress, for the business to become profitable it will have to deliver 400,000 vehicles annually. So far, its workers have never pushed annual production beyond 100,000.

Musk, however, is thinking beyond workers.

The future is total automation.

During the Gilded Age, the assembly line transformed industrial production. This is a New Gilded Age. It is about information technology: intelligent software, sensors, and incredibly precise, fast-moving robotics. These technologies promise exponential improvement in production.

Humans, at least those who fasten bolts or shift metal, become superfluous.

It's not science fiction. Musk, ever the salesman, has big plans for factories that are unencumbered by the physical limitations of humans.

In Tesla's July 2016 mission statement he wrote about his epiphany: turning the factory into a machine. He even gave it a cool name: "Alien Dreadnought"—a machine that makes machines.

By his math, Dreadnought version 3.0 could improve production by 5x to 10x. That's still a few years away. Through mid-2018, however, he was still working on version 0.5. It began with the initial production of the Model 3. Musk promises version 1.0 will come in 2019 when new equipment hits the factory floors.

In November 2016, Tesla bought Grohmann Engineering, a German automation specialist. Since then, the company has been working to implement the cutting edge gear. The ramp up to 2,000 Model 3s is the first evidence the strategy is bearing fruit.

With 580 giant, robotic arms, the Freemont factory was already state-of-the-art. Massive mechanical arms push human limits. From 2012 through November 2016, the plant had a 400 percent increase in production. And workers—the human kind—have complained often about the frantic pace.

Newer versions of Dreadnought will supersede their frailties. Robots will move so quickly and so efficiently that humans won't be safe on the factory floors. Only a skeleton staff of engineers will be on hand—and they will merely monitor production.

This would represent the first major advance in automobile manufacturing since Toyota introduced the *just in time* approach in 1992. Then, the premise was to produce cars on an as-needed basis, with minimum waste and maximum automation.

Automation and cutting-edge robotics are upping the ante. With greater computing power, data analytics, and advanced modeling software, most outcomes can be predetermined. It's a new industrial revolution. It will lead to unimagined profitability and huge new opportunities for investors.

Dreadnought is the first step. Eliminating most humans, at least in theory, would improve production by orders of magnitude.

Engineering would be the sole arbiter of production. Raw materials would enter factories at one end. Finished cars would emerge from the other end.

It's easy to want to bet against Musk. Automobile factory floors are already full of complex machines. The Robotics Industries Association estimates that 265,000 robots are already working in US factories. The consensus holds that all the potential efficiencies have been exploited.

However, Musk is ambitious and talented. He is also in a hurry to get places.

He came up with a feasible plan for Hyperloop—a way to whisk passengers though a vacuum tube at 760 mph. His rocket company can deliver satellites to orbit, then return them to Earth with pinpoint accuracy. His electric cars are safe and green and can blow away a Lamborghini.

He is used to doing what most people consider impossible. If he can pull off the Alien Dreadnought, the face of manufacturing will change forever.

Investors have the opportunity to participate by buying the tools that will make it all possible.

Industrial Robots, Made in Japan

Long before there was Dreadnought, Japanese engineers dreamed of the ultimate unnamed factory.

Yaskawa Electric Corp. is a Japanese company founded in 1915 by Keiichiro Yasukawa, the son of a prominent samurai. Yasukawa built a substantial business supplying industrial motors for the coal mining industry. Over the years it has grown into an industrial powerhouse.

In 1958, its engineers built a cutting-edge DC servomotor. It was so successful that they envisioned the unmanned factory, where the motors would be continuously produced, with human workers serving only as overseers. The ambition to get to that unmanned factory spurred other innovations.

The company introduced Mechantronics in 1969. The idea was to fuse electric motors and mechanical machines. It led to the world's first general purpose transistor AC drive. The birth of the modern robot, the Motoman, followed.

In 1990, Yaskawa Electric opened the first factory in the world that used automated robots to build other automated robots. Its first factory, at Kitakyushu headquarters, still produces light-use robots and heavy-duty arc welders.

In keeping with the long history, both are Motoman.

Today Motoman robots are prevalent on the factory, warehouse, cleanroom, and laboratory floors worldwide. The Motoman MPX 3500 handles high-performance painting tasks in the automotive industry. CSDA 10 is deployed across the cosmetics and biomedical industries. MotoSense is the laser welder and cutter of choice in light manufacturing, and GP Series robots can be found in semiconductor labs throughout Asia.

And Yaskawa is only getting started.

More powerful networks, robust cloud computing infrastructure, and millions of sensors are coming to transform its core business. Motoman robots will get real-time analytics and artificial intelligence as they move forward with Industry 4.0 initiatives. They will be better, stronger, faster.

Like the six million dollar man, without any human frailties.

The Georg Fischer Fittings is an Austrian metal fabricator. The company produces 12,200 tons of malleable fittings annually for export to the European Union and Switzerland. Its threaded cast iron cap manufacturing consists of four Motoman robots, one Motoman DX200 controller system, a camera system with six cameras, and the MotoPlus software developer kit interface.

The metal pieces move along a conveyor belt where they are scanned for imperfections by the camera system, before being sorted and fed into the turning station by robots. After being machined and threaded, a part is scanned again for imperfection. Then it is sorted into a bin as the finished product.

Four finished parts are produced every 20 seconds. No humans are involved in the process. And the robots can be retooled in one hour. The sensors feed data to the software SDK, which in turn drives the Motomans. Everything is in sync, resulting in greater productivity and less waste.

The applications for robotics and Industry 4.0 are endless. Yaskawa is planning to expand its smart robotic empire to care for the elderly and the search for new drugs.

After many false starts, the manufacturers are finally beginning to see the value proposition in smart machines.

In November 2016, IDC, a global research firm, estimated that by 2020, 40 percent of commercial robots will be connected to a mesh of shared intelligence, resulting in a 200 percent improvement in operational efficiency.

HOW TO PLAY: Yaskawa is the industry leader. The shares peaked in early 2018 and pulled back 50 percent over the summer in sync with tightening business conditions in Japan. However, once shares stabilize, they should make a good bet on the trend toward smart robotics.

The Future of Spinal Surgery

In science fiction movies, surgeries are always performed by robots. The science part is still true. The fiction is no more. Surgical robots are here.

Mazor Robotics (MZOR) makes surgical robots that must be seen to be believed. Its Mazor X platform combines data analytics, 3D imaging, and cutting-edge robotics to help surgeons perform the most delicate of spinal and brain procedures with remarkable precision.

Now the install base is surging. And an important partnership is kicking into gear.

The Israeli company was founded in 2001 by Moshe Shoham, a professor of mechanical engineering at Technion, and Eli Zehavi, a former vice president of engineering at Elscint. By 2004 they had built SpineAssist, the first commercial guidance system for spine surgery.

The early success attracted **Medtronic** (MDT), the giant medical device company. However, the current platform is light years ahead of its early devices. Its Renaissance surgical arm, developed in 2011, takes robotic surgery assurance to the next level.

An integrated 3D camera uses spatial tracking to map the pre-operation surface and surrounding area. Fluoroscopic images taken with 3D markers build surgical plans. Sophisticated algorithms govern the robotic arm, translating the surgical plan with pinpoint accuracy.

It all seems like something from a crazy efficient future.

The industry is taking note. With the help of Medtronic, Mazor has 170 installations on four continents. Surgeons have assisted 27,000 patients, and 190,000 screws and other implants have been precisely placed.

In an August 2017 investor presentation, the company noted it expects to reach almost 5,000 procedures and 113 installations in the United States alone, in fiscal 2017. These numbers represent 52 percent growth over fiscal 2016.

The second phase of its deal with Medtronic will bring exclusive global sales and support, annual minimum targets, and a commitment to noncompete.

It's a win for Medtronic, Mazor, and operating rooms. The platform reduces complications and failures over freehand procedures. In the high stakes world of modern medicine, that is time and money. It's also something that can be easily sold.

There are rewards due Mazor shareholders, too. As its deal with Medtronic transitions to phase 2, employees and marketing costs will shift to the larger company. Mazor believes this will lead to a decline in operating costs from 124 percent of sales in 2016 to 45 percent by 2020.

Revenues have been very steady. Through fiscal 2017, sales reached $233 million, up 67 percent over fiscal 2016 and a threefold increase over the 2013 results.

Its shares have begun to reflect the strong growth and substantial potential. The Mazor X is the leading robotics platform in its category. Installations and patients served are growing steadily. These trends should accelerate as its partner, Medtronic, seeks more market penetration. In 2016, the stock rallied 115 percent. That was followed by gains of 135 percent during 2017.

Ultimately, this is the future of complex surgery. Just like in the movies.

Success with Fewer Tiny Cuts

Intuitive Surgical (ISRG) started with a very simple plan: make surgery less invasive by using smart, agile robots. In 1995, the concept seemed far-fetched.

Researchers at the Stanford Research Institute had been kicking around the idea for years. They were under contract by the US Army. The big idea was remote battlefield surgery. In theory, a surgeon could be anywhere and still save the lives of wounded soldiers.

By 1994, the SRI system caught the attention of Frederic Moll, an executive at Guidant. Among other medical products, the Indianapolis company made a range of tiny wires, balloons, and catheters favored by the healthcare industry to repair clogged arteries. The devices were cost effective and less invasive than heart surgery. For Moll, the SRI robotic system was not so much a technological marvel as it was another way to make surgery less invasive.

Moll put together a business plan and pitched it to Guidant brass. They rejected it.

In 1995, Moll, met John Freund and Robert Younge. The two men were veterans of Acuson, the company behind the first fully computerized ultrasound system. Freund quickly negotiated the intellectual property rights for the SRI system. A business plan followed, and the three men began to raise seed capital.

Intuitive Surgical was born.

Five years later, in 2000, the company raised $46 million

with an initial public offering. It was the same year the Food and Drug Administration allowed Intuitive Surgical robotic systems, now called da Vinci, for use in general laparoscopic surgery. In 2001, da Vinci was given the green light for prostate cancer surgery.

Since that time, Moll left the company, but da Vinci became the gold standard in robotic surgery. Today, the system is in use for a host of cardiac and gynecological procedures. The attraction is the size of the incision. da Vinci continues to be much less invasive than traditional surgery.

And the company has benefitted handsomely from advances in information technology. da Vinci has become a connected platform, where surgeons train and practice their skills, using the latest tools. There is even a virtual reality simulator.

Its Endowrist instruments are fully robotic "wrists" attached to four robotic arms. The wrists are designed with seven degrees of motion, to perfectly clamp, cut, coagulate, dissect, suture, and manipulate tissue far better than the human hand. And da Vinci software uses predictive analytics to continuously autocorrect tremors, while precisely translating the surgeon's gestures.

The company claims that every 36 seconds, somewhere in the world, da Vinci helps a surgeon to perform better. As of the end of 2017, that has led to success with five million patients, 43,000 trained surgeons, and 4,989 systems installed at 100 percent of the top hospitals for cancer, gynecology, gastroenterology, and urology.

Intuitive Surgical has 2,700 patents, and 1,900 pending.

The company also gets as much as $170,000 in recurring service revenue per installation and $3,200 per use. In 2017, that worked out to $573 million and $1.64 billion, respectively, or 71 percent of sales. That's a good business.

And the company is looking forward. In addition to robotics, it's making significant research and development investments in artificial intelligence to ensure it's not disrupted by some start-up that wants to bring autonomous or remote location surgery to the masses.

The company operates a dominant franchise in a fast-growing sector. It logged 15.8 percent sales growth in 2017, on $3.1 billion in sales, and its market penetration in Europe and Asia is only getting started. At four times sales, the shares are not cheap, but the company is growing fast. Buy the stock on pullbacks.

The Robotics of Food

You probably never give a second thought to the machinery required to package cookies, vacuum seal meats, and can soda, juices, and vegetables. Why would you? Packaging does not seem to be important.

John Bean Technologies (JBT) is the dominant robotics player in every facet of the food business. Among other things, its machines package cookies, vacuum seal meats, and can soda, juices, and vegetables. When food companies build new factories, they call JBT.

They're calling a lot. Traditional factories are being retrofitted with smart technologies to improve productivity. The Internet of Things revolution is here. And JBT is ready.

BI Intelligence expects the number of IoT devices to swell from 237 million in 2015 to more than 923 million in 2020. By the same year, global manufacturers should spend a staggering $267 billion for tracking assets, consolidating their control structures, and implementing data analytics to improve predictive maintenance, Business Insider reports.

JBT management saw it all coming years ago.

Working with the likes of Campbell Soup, Coca Cola, Dole Foods, Florida Natural Growers, General Mills, AgroSuper SA, and others, it had the inside track.

It invested aggressively in research and development. In 2016, JBT boosted investment by 30 percent. According to Thomas Giacomini, president and CEO, it is money well spent. Smarter machines mean better yields and less down time. They also mean "maximizing profits for our customers," he says.

There is another benefit.

The fastest growing region in the world is Asia. China, in particular, is anxious to upgrade its factories with state-of-the-art gear.

In food processing, JBT is the only company with the scale to play there. And it has been bulking up with a new innovation center and a customer outreach program.

John Bean Technologies is also investing in automatic guided vehicles. Now it's committed to making all those machines smarter with IoT sensors and software.

To listen to Giacomini, the evolution was never in doubt. Among other things, JBT machines zip around warehouse floors; extract juices from fruits and vegetables; vacuum seal meats; seal cans; and cook, coat, freeze, and portion control processed foods. Making the machines and processes smarter just made good business sense.

"It means we can proactively identify and diagnose issues, improving yields, throughput and uptime, maximizing profits for our customers," Giacomini told analysts during a conference call.

Still, automating warehouses and food processing plants is not exactly revolutionary. What separates JBT from its competitors is scale.

It's dominant in every part of the food sector and constantly on the lookout for new technologies. JBT recently completed the acquisition of Cooling and Applied Technologies and Tipper Tie. The deals reinforce its lead in poultry processing and packaging.

Consulting firm IDC Research predicts worldwide spending for robotics will swell to $135 billion by 2019. The bulk of new growth will be discrete and process manufacturing. And Asia/Pacific is expected to comprise 65 percent of robotics spending.

This certainly jibes with JBT's strategy. Giacomini believes the growing Asian middle class will seek more value-added food. To get ready, JBT bulked up its team in the region and opened an innovation center in China, where it's aggressively engaging potential clients.

Meanwhile, the company is looking for another strong year in 2017. Revenue growth is expected to rise 15 percent on the basis of 3–5 percent organic growth and 11 percent from acquisitions.

Leading food processing companies are only beginning to modernize their plants and equipment with the tools of the digital era. JBT is one of the best pure plays in that space.

HOW TO PLAY: Yaskawa Electric Corp., Mazor Robotics, Intuitive Surgical, and John Bean Technologies are not household names. These companies are niche players. They operate at the cutting edge of the industrial, medical, and food processing worlds. Their gear is networked, and they exploit advanced data analytics and AI. And each company has a substantial patent portfolio. That gives the companies pricing power and a big lead on the rest of the pack.

Fast Forward

The robot apocalypse is real. Humans are in peril, but not in the way that most fear. Robots are getting smarter every day, and they are coming for human jobs. The key is software, as robots' intelligence has finally begun to match their physical dexterity.

Most of the rise of smart robots is convergence. Networks, sensors, cloud-based data analytics, and artificial intelligence have transformed real-world robots into thinking machines. Sensors allow these machines to see, hear, feel, and even measure to make sense of the surrounding environment. And they are relentless. Except for maintenance, robots never go off-line or demand paternity leave or go on vacation or suffer mental breakdowns.

In the industrial world, they have been implemented as painters and spot welders. In retail they are price checkers, warehouse shelf movers, and autonomous forklift operators. But that is just a small fraction of their capability. Soon, they will work in search and rescue operations in the most dangerous places on Earth. They will assist surgeons, help amputees regain the use of lost limbs, and care for the elderly.

CHAPTER 8

BLOCKCHAIN: THE TRANSPARENCY REVOLUTION

Bankers and anarchists. Blockchain makes strange bedfellows. Then again, a system that promises to squash fraud while diminishing the power of global elites is going to attract a wide swath of believers. Blockchain, as a technology, is in that space.

In this chapter I will show how the foundational ledger system for bitcoin became a panacea for the masses. I will discuss its inherent strengths and show many of the most exciting applications and new business models that are developing. And I will shine a light on two mature businesses that are set to grab a big piece of the inevitable windfall.

Hackers' Worst Nightmare

Very soon, hundreds of billions of things will be connected to networks. Nefarious hackers are giddy with anticipation.

Sounds dangerous, but don't worry too much. White-hat network architects are plotting too. They plan to foil hackers with a technology called *blockchain*.

In the early stages of ultra-connectivity, attaching sensors to big cloud-based networks was expensive but rewarding work. Networkers and clients reaped huge rewards by continuously monitoring jet engines and implementing smart meter systems to track power and water consumption in factories. It was a win-win situation. Then it all changed. The culprit was trust. How could networkers be certain their clients' valuable data had not been compromised?

In the early part of 2014, **IBM** set out on a new path. It devised a plan in which clients surrendered some control over the ecosystem and data in exchange for trust.

The new model involved blockchain, an open ledger system using peer-to-peer computing.

While clients were intrigued by the notion of greater trust, they were also reluctant to give up control of data, especially to a ledger that had its roots in the much maligned cryptocurrency known as bitcoin.

The strength of blockchain is transparency. Because it is a permanent record that can never be erased or altered, every participant knows exactly what's happening at all times. Collective verification through distributed consensus removes the need for trusted third parties such as banks, insurers, and lawyers.

The benefits are immediately obvious. In theory, blockchain eliminates even the possibility of fraud. It is cost effective and frictionless. And, because it is decentralized and encrypted, no entity can exert control over the system. That makes it infinitely scalable and future proof.

It sounds too good to be true. But it is. In theory.

Imagine a world where smart devices become participants on the blockchain as they become operational. Distributed consensus allows them to independently and safely complete transactions in their self-interest with other entities living on the blockchain.

A smart TV could accept a software update from its manufacturer based on that transaction being verified on the blockchain. A self-driving car could diagnose, schedule, and even pay for its own maintenance. Vending machines could monitor stock and solicit bids for replacement. Automatically.

There is more. Connected home appliances could engage each other to determine the best use schedule to minimize electricity costs.

All of these complex operations are made possible by many smaller completed blocks of transactions on the larger chain.

Best of all, it's impossible for hackers to intervene because there's no way to verify malicious code on the blockchain.

There are some natural obstacles to this new world order. The transparent, trustless, and inherently low-cost nature of blockchain means traditional middlemen and their requisite big fees are cut out of the loop.

Blockchain is bad news for lawyers, bankers, and accountants.

There is also the question of compute costs. Decentralization means many computers are required to verify transactions. The cost of maintaining these computers must have functional value.

But these are little things. Blockchain is a solution for inherent trust issues. It is uniquely transparent and decentralized.

Origins of the Blockchain

To fully understand blockchain, and how important is it going to be, you have to understand where it came from, and where it is headed.

Bitcoin, the most prominent cryptocurrency, was born in 2008 when a white paper authored under pseudonym Satoshi Nakamoto appeared on a cryptography mailing list. The big idea was a better electronic payment system through the use of cryptography.

Nakamoto's concept was sound. The underlying code was completely open source. The ledger system, blockchain, was transparent and permanent. As a reward for maintaining the ledger, coins are "mined" into existence through computer-assisted cryptography. The peer-to-peer network structure meant anonymity and no central authority.

In January 2009, the first 50 coins were mined.

Bitcoin came into existence at a significant moment in history. The financial crisis gripped the entire world. Stock indexes had plummeted. Wall Street institutions failed. Confidence in traditional fiat currencies, as a store of value, seemed more vulnerable than at any point in modern history.

Bitcoin brought hard and fast rules. It brought transactional transparency.

At the time, it seemed the perfect response to the instability of the central banking apparatus. Most people believe the money they earn, save, and invest is backed by hard currency, like gold. In reality, the supply of paper is unlimited.

It only has value because it is supported by the government that issued it. In contrast, the limit for bitcoin is 21 million coins. They cannot be duplicated, manipulated, or forged because it is the product of a blockchain with complete transparency. And no one party or government controls bitcoin. It is the product of a distributed trustless consensus.

In that context, the inherent value of bitcoin as a store of value becomes more clear.

In 2017, cryptocurrency investing hit the mainstream in a big way. During the year, the price of bitcoin rose to $13,286, a thirteenfold increase from its price a year earlier. The strength sparked alternative coins and public fascination.

Behind the scenes, financial services IT developers were wondering how Satoshi Nakamoto managed to get so much right. Forget bitcoin: With blockchain as the foundation, a group of part-time hackers managed to cobble together a robust, scalable, and encrypted payment infrastructure that eradicated the need for financial intermediaries.

The financial services sector, even with its $500 million in combined annual IT spending, had not come close to accomplishing this.

The spigots opened. Start-ups all over the globe began developing blockchains. Alliances were formed. In September 2015, an alliance of nine financial companies formed R3. Two weeks later, 13 additional companies joined. As of March 2018, the network of members extended to more than 200 banks, financial institutions, regulators, and developers.

In March 2017, The Enterprise Ethereum Alliance was founded to connect developers, academics, technology vendors, and Fortune 500 enterprises working on the Ethereum blockchain, a forked version of the bitcoin original. What makes Ethereum special is smart contracts.

Smart contracts are tiny computer programs that can be built into the Ethereum blockchain. These bits of code allow individuals, machines, and software code to enter and complete transactions. That means the contracts become part of the ledger forever, making them transparent.

In March 2018, Marsh & McLennan, the giant insurance broker, joined EAA, bringing the total number of companies to over 400. More join every week.

Some of the rush is about fear of disruption. Some of it is excitement for the future. There is no telling what is possible with blockchain.

Blockchain at Sea

What do Somalian pirates, oranges, pineapples, and Chinese pork bellies have in common? They are all in the crosshairs of a new technology that promises to change the supply chain.

In January 2018, IBM and Maersk, the world's largest marine cargo shipping company, announced they would use blockchain to improve cargo tracking and reduce fraud and the time products spend sitting in ports.

Blockchain brings transparency. Participants see the entire supply chain, end-to-end in real time. All of those prying eyes and encryption mean transactions cannot be tampered with or easily deleted. In theory, it's foolproof.

"That was the 'aha' for me. This was not really about digital payments, but establishing trust in transactions in general," Arvind Krishna, director of research at IBM, told the *New York Times*. "[It is] a technology that can change the world."

So far, it's been mostly about streamlining red tape and reducing fraud.

In the case of Maersk, the task is mammoth. The company ships millions of rectangular containers all over the world every year. Each has a paper trail handled by up to 30 different customs, tax, and health organizations. A single lost document can cause an entire ship laden with thousands of containers to sit idle in port for days.

Maersk says fully one-fifth of the cost of shipping is red tape. The potential savings is in the billions of dollars.

And then there is fraud. While North Africa is still rife with actual seafaring Somalian pirates, many have gone white-collar. The *bill of lading* is the legal receipt shippers use to document product delivery. Unfortunately, it's also the most tampered with and copied document in the entire supply chain.

Forged documents lead to billions of dollars of stolen and counterfeited goods.

Blockchain and digitalization reduce or remove this possibility. All documents become part of the chain. Nobody can delete or change the record without the consensus of the entire network. The only end-around would be a system hack. Advanced cryptography makes that almost impossible.

Walmart is one of 400 clients trialing IBM's blockchain. In October 2017 it began using the open-source software to track Chinese pork throughout the supply chain—from producers to processors to distributors to grocers to consumers. Each step left an indelible record.

Maersk reports successful trials tracking mandarin oranges shipped from California, and pineapples sent from Columbia to the port of Rotterdam in the Netherlands.

The International Chamber of Shipping reports 90 percent of world trade is carried by the international shipping industry. More than 50,000 vessels are afloat, representing 150 nations at any given time. The potential impact of blockchain is enormous.

In theory, developers can use blockchain to digitally sign

every transaction along the journey. It would eliminate the need for trust and the need for countless intermediaries. It would cut the cost of shipping exponentially.

The savings would boost world economic growth.

Blockchain for Refugees

By 2030, the United Nations wants everyone on the planet to have a digital identity. It's an enormous task.

Microsoft and **Accenture** have been tinkering with blockchain schemes for years. So far, their interest has been about financial technology.

Now they have an ambitious prototype that could give a digital blockchain ID to each of the 1.1 billion people who don't have documented proof of their existence.

These people—who account for about one-sixth of the world's population—live in social limbo. Consequently, they are excluded from many social, political, economic, educational, and health programs. A secure, fast, and flexible blockchain could be the solution to bringing these people into the world community.

It is also an opportunity for investors. Documenting more than a billion people living in the shadows would showcase the technology on a world stage. It would legitimize new platforms and open up new use cases.

Bankers know this. That is why they have been falling all over each other to invest in platforms.

They see the potential to eliminate costly back-office operations. They see low-latency transactions and reduced counterparty risks. It's banker nirvana: fatter profits, less fraud, and fewer people shuffling papers.

It's ironic the same technology might also solve the myriad problems that face refugees and their host countries. Driven from their homes by war or natural disasters, refugees often arrive in camps with little more than the clothes on their backs.

Without adequate IDs, it's difficult for refugees to start new lives. Without uniform IDs for refugees, it's difficult for aid workers to provide adequate services fairly.

To solve the problem, Accenture and Microsoft have joined to support ID2020, a program to give people digital identities. The program will use a secure database to store anonymously collected biometric data like fingerprints, iris, and facial scans. Then blockchain will link each individual's data to a unique identifier. As people receive services, like healthcare, they collect digital stamps that are linked to that identifier.

It's a win for all involved. Refugees get a dependable personal identity record. Host nations get a reliable account of services provided at distinct locations. Accenture gets to show off their biometric software platform. And Microsoft gets to tout the flexibility and scalability of Azure Cloud, its giant cloud-computing platform.

There is a lot of buzz about blockchain. The prospect of a completely transparent, decentralized digital ledger led PricewaterhouseCoopers, the global accounting and consulting firm, to call blockchain a once-in-a-generation opportunity.

In a 2016 research report, PWC highlighted the possibility for a new breed of low-latency, smart financial contracts capable of self-executing. The cost savings would be staggering.

These instruments would remove the middlemen, literally.

Irving Wladawsky-Berger, an MIT lecturer and early IBM technology maven, went even further. He called blockchain the next major step in the evolution of the Internet. He reasons that the Internet is great, but doing business online still requires a large leap of faith.

Finding the right thingamabob on Amazon.com is easy. But entering your credit card information means trusting the information is not being intercepted, and that the online retailer will keep it safe.

With security and transparency, blockchain overcomes these limitations.

With all of the praise, you might think hordes of investors would be all over blockchain. Nothing could be further from the truth. Most investors are missing it. They believe it's too complicated, too esoteric.

But blockchain is happening. It's being mobilized in myriad ways, and a number of public companies have established important footholds.

Accenture is building a massive platform and attracting all the right partners in financial services. **Microsoft** is pushing the technology to its logical limits. It is abstracting the ledger system to a fee-for-service. The digital and physical worlds are merging with a blockchain dose of checks and balances.

And that is just the start. Possibilities exist in biotech, natural resources, and the military, too. The time to add positions in the development is now. The potential market is enormous.

Blockchain Can Unshackle Banking

Bankers are under attack around the world. The assault is not being led by masked men with pistols but rather by anonymous cyber thieves armed with malicious code.

The bankers' vulnerability stems from a historic shift.

Before 1973, the world's banks had a communication problem. Transferring money involved countless phone calls, telex machine messages, and frustration. Bankers needed to take control of the process.

Thus was born the member-owned message system, Society for Worldwide Interbank Financial Telecommunication.

For more than four decades, the SWIFT system has standardized the global bank messaging system, allowing institutions to transfer funds and letters of credit as well as to make security transactions quickly and securely. In 2015, operating out of data centers in Belgium and the United States, SWIFT counted more than 11,000 member institutions in 200 countries and routed 24 million messages daily using unique 8- or 11-character codes.

Although SWIFT held no member funds, bankers came to rely on the automated message system. It seemed beyond reproach until details leaked about a cyber heist at the Bangladesh Central Bank where thieves had penetrated the SWIFT system and looted member banks.

The Bangladesh heist was a wake-up call to the industry. Using stolen security credentials on February 4, 2016, hackers sent three dozen fraudulent money transfer requests to the Federal Reserve Bank of New York. The US bank was directed to send $951 million from the Bangladesh Central Bank account to recipients in Sri Lanka, the Philippines, and other parts of Asia.

The Bangladesh bank managed to block 30 transfers worth $851 million when the messages were flagged for syntax errors. Twenty million was later recovered from Sri Lanka. The remaining $81 million was successfully routed to the Philippines.

In May 2016, cyber thieves attacked a Vietnamese bank. It was a clear indication that an orchestrated campaign targeting SWIFT-member banks was underway. In both cases, thieves stole the SWIFT credentials of member banks.

When crooks saw money transferred to other banks held in the member account name, they submitted fraudulent messages asking that money be transferred back to one of their own accounts.

To cover their tracks, the thieves used malware code. In the Bangladesh robbery, the bandits submitted messages asking for more than $1 billion before eventually making off with $81 million.

These cases are not isolated. Russian cyber security firm Kaspersky Lab claims Interpol and other agencies estimate that more than $1 billion has been pilfered from 100 financial institutions during the last two years by the Carbanak cyber gang spread across Russia, Ukraine, and China.

The SWIFT weaknesses are fodder for calls to overhaul the banking system with something far more robust. Ironically, getting there will involve surrendering the control member firms sought when they created SWIFT in Brussels decades ago.

Bankers are betting that blockchain is the solution.

Forty-two of the largest banks, including **Goldman Sachs**, **J.P. Morgan**, **Citigroup**, **Wells Fargo**, and **Bank of America**, have already begun testing blockchain solutions. The motivation is largely economic.

The banks believe blockchain will lead to annual back office cost savings of $20 billion. Stumping cyber criminals would be an extra benefit. Blockchain will directly improve adopting banks' bottom lines. Bankers like that—a lot.

HOW TO PLAY: Leaders in developing blockchain solutions for banks are Accenture and Microsoft.

Centralizing the Decentralized Blockchain

A pair of ex-Google employees believes their version of blockchain can fix banking, too.

Paul Taylor and Will Montgomery have a history of building sophisticated software. Taylor developed speech-text code at Phonetics Arts. That company was acquired by Google in 2010, and its transformative seed is still evolving throughout the ecosystem. Montgomery is one of the engineers who brought Adsense, Google's commerce engine, to prominence.

Together they formed Thought Machine and have been working with a team of 50 engineers for the past two years on a platform they call Vault OS.

Vault aims to help banks communicate with one another with a future-proof, flexible implementation of blockchain. The concept is simple: Because blockchain is transparent, everyone can see what's happening with the chain at every moment in the life of the transaction. All of those metaphorical peering eyes and cryptography should eliminate the possibility of fraud and speed-up transactions.

What makes Vault unlike a normal blockchain is centralization. In most blockchains, nobody has direct control over the chain. Instead, transactions are completed by a number of unrelated computer systems.

Vault OS will live inside Thought Machine's network of cloud-based servers.

While ceding responsibility is a bit of a gamble for normally risk adverse bankers, Thought Machine is offering plenty in return. In addition to keeping banks current with regulatory requirements, the company promises an end to embarrassing information technology snafus, and new functionality that lets banks offer personalized customer products.

For example, a customer could tell the software to build a loan that increases mortgage payments automatically in months when spending is otherwise reduced.

Thought Machine compares this idea to Nike ID that allows customers to choose the colors and materials of their bespoke shoes.

Taylor and Montgomery know getting bankers to buy into their fix is an uphill battle. However, given the stakes, the time is right for a transition.

When the financial services industry flocked to the SWIFT message system in the 1970s, few of them could have imagined hackers who would develop malicious software to rob untold millions.

Fewer still would have believed member firms would respond by experimenting with nonproprietary software. It's a brave new world for criminals and for the people trying to stay one step ahead.

Porsche Speeds into the Blockchain Era

A fully loaded Porsche Panamera 4S Executive will run you $147,750 before taxes. And soon, its software will be powered by blockchain.

In February 2017, the German luxury sports carmaker said it was working with XAIN, a Berlin-based start-up, to bring a distributed ledger system to its high-end vehicles.

It makes sense. Future cars will be data centers on wheels. Blockchain platforms may be the best way to keep information safe, while making possible cool new features.

XAIN was founded by Leif-Nissen Lundbaek, as a follow-up to his PhD thesis at Imperial College in London, and his master's project at Oxford University. Today, he leads a 17-person start-up with offices in Berlin and London. XAIN engineers are building an artificially intelligent network on top of a private Ethereum blockchain.

It's complex. But the substance is that XAIN is using AI to detect anomalies, to make the platform stable, robust, and scalable for applications like automobiles.

Modern high-end cars are already complicated. They have advanced driver-assistance systems that automatically jam on the brakes or self-steer if the driver becomes distracted. They have complicated infotainment packages that sync with smartphones and satellite systems. And many are continually connected to monitoring networks.

All of these features generate massive amounts of digital data. Today, much of that information is not secure.

Blockchain is a remedy. It is also a way to get ready for future vehicles that will be connected, self-driving, and full of features that now seem like science fiction.

XAIN's test Panamera is packed with innovative features. In addition to secure data logging, the owner can remotely share the vehicle key or view the security access online. An owner might send an access code to FedEx so a delivery person could open the trunk lid and drop off a parcel. Or a car-sharing service might send a virtual key to a renter.

In both cases, the transactions are completed on the blockchain. The participants get a near instant confirmation that is forever trackable. It is secure, highly efficient, and cost effective.

In the future, XAIN executives foresee its blockchain technology being used to verify data for over-the-air vehicle software updates, self-driving, and connected features.

> **HOW TO PLAY:** These sorts of projects are also gathering a lot of attention at networking hardware pioneer and industry behemoth **Cisco Systems** (CSCO). As part of the Enterprise Ethereum Alliance, the San Jose company is using smart contracts and blockchain to secure networks of connected things. It's a good buy on pullbacks to take advantage of this change in the industry.

A Blockchain Leader Emerges: Microsoft

It's hard enough to believe that Microsoft is a cloud-computer company. It's even harder to believe the company is now pushing forward aggressively with plans to take a leadership role in blockchain, a technology that did not exist a decade ago.

In mid-2017, the Redmond technology giant laid off thousands as it moved from selling boxed software to cloud-based solutions. It's an ironic twist for the company responsible for moving computing to desktops.

That's fine. The cloud and its services are the future.

In 2016 Gartner, an independent research group, predicted a $1 trillion shift in IT spending to the cloud. While Microsoft embraced the cloud long ago, it became its future when Satya Nadella replaced Steve Ballmer as CEO in 2014.

By 2017, Nadella announced targeted layoffs of 2,850, with 900 boxed sales workers getting pink slips. They were replaced by 1,000 employees with experience selling cloud-based products.

The results have been stunning. In January 2017, *Bloomberg* reported sales at Azure, its cloud-computing business, nearly doubled. Customers for Office 365, the cloud-based productivity suite, pushed beyond 25 million. Microsoft says it will reach $20 billion in annualized revenue from the cloud by the end of 2018.

The Microsoft plan is to offer better services than its competitors, AWS and Google Cloud. It starts with Blockchain-as-a-Service built into Azure. And Microsoft has been busily building turnkey applications and forging alliances with key players.

In 2017, the company started a marketplace for blockchain solutions. It's a one-stop market for open-source technologies needed to piece together blockchain applications. Developers can use distributed ledgers from Corda, Hyperledger, and Ethereum to get code running in minutes.

In November 2017, the Monetary Authority of Singapore, in partnership with R3, was able to build an Azure blockchain for the settlement of securities and payments. Although the project is still in the proof-of-concept stage, it is a major milestone as the work toward a digital form of the Singapore dollar.

Singapore is often considered the most digitally forward country in the world. It has plans for a full smart city effort, and tokenized currency is a big part of the way forward.

In June 2017, Accenture, KPMG, and a consortium of Indian banks signed on with Azure.

Members and the Bankchain consortium—State Bank of India, ICICI bank, Kotah Bank, Bank of Baroda, Deutsche Bank and many others—will use Microsoft Azure exclusively for their blockchain solutions. This includes anti–money laundering, know your customer, and anti-terrorism.

In a March 2018 report, "From Buzz to Bucks, Automotive Players On the Highway to Car Data Monetization," McKinsey & Co. says the connected car market may be worth $450 to $750 billion by 2030.

Microsoft revealed a major connected car platform in January 2017. Since then it has announced partnerships with Renault Nissan and Tata Motors, the parent company of Jaguar and Land Rover.

And in March 2017, company officials announced the licensing of its portfolio of connected car patents to Toyota.

Cars connected to the Azure network will seamlessly share information to avoid traffic and enhance safety through assisted driver systems and predictive maintenance. These vehicles will also provide the comforts of home and office to passengers. Blockchain could play an important role in making sure everything runs smoothly with smart contracts.

It's no wonder, in March 2016, PricewaterhouseCoopers called Blockchain a once in a generation opportunity.

Microsoft is establishing a foothold in all of these technologies. And it's happening because the company courageously looked past its old business and embraced the cloud and the new technologies it made possible.

This is a gigantic opportunity for the company. It is well positioned. It has the right partners, with deep reach into large enterprises. And best of all, this is just getting started. This is a stock that can be bought into any substantial weakness.

Cisco Rediscovers Its Soul in Blockchain

In the golden era of the Internet, let's call it 1995 to 2010, demand for **Cisco Systems** (CSCO) switches, hubs, and routers was insatiable. In March 2000, it was the most valuable company in the world.

The reach of the Internet is still growing. But lately, it has been growing away from the company that Leonard Bosack and Sandy Lerner built in 1984. Centralized public clouds are the new networks, and increasingly, they are using virtualization to abstract away the hardware that made Cisco a household name.

Connected devices on the edge of the network and blockchain offer a way back.

Nobody doubts these devices are coming. Sensors have been commoditized. We are wearing them. They are in our vehicles. They are being deployed on factory floors and city streets. Right now, all of that digital data is being collected and sent back to the network where it is crunched by powerful data analytic software. Lately, analysts have become skeptical about the economics of centralized processing.

In mid-2017, Forrester Research, an international information technology research firm, warned clients that data overload makes it "increasingly uneconomical to do all of the processing centrally." It's far more efficient and practical to process data where it is collected.

This is called *edge computing*. Data gets processed as close to the source as possible— the edge of the network—instead of in massive data-storage warehouses.

You can already see how the process has been pushed to the edge of networks. New iPhones use special chips to keep authentication data on the device and off of Apple servers. It speeds up processing, and it's a big privacy bonus. Nvidia is taking edge computing to the extreme by building supercomputers for self-driving cars. The Drive PX Pegasus can process 320 million instructions per second.

Reducing latency by a few seconds on a smartphone certainly improves the user experience. However, in a self-driving car, going 55 mph on a crowded road, those seconds could be the difference between life and death.

And there are many similar implementations. Think about fast-moving robotic arms in industrial factories, heavy machinery in mining pits or on oil rigs, or smart grids to manage traffic.

Cisco has been preparing for this new era of connected devices and edge computing for a long time. Since 2012, the company has been a serial acquirer of IoT assets. Security was the first focus. Since 2012, Cisco bought Open DNS, Sourcefire, Neohapsis, ThreatGRID, Portcullis, and Virtuata. In September 2014, Metacloud, a start-up focused on building secure cloud platforms for the IoT, was acquired. In 2015, Cisco began folding IoT data analytics companies like ParStream, Lancope, and MaintenanceNet into the mix.

Then, in February 2016, the company bought Jasper Technologies, the leading IoT service platform. Jasper runs the connective tissue for the world's biggest automotive, aircraft, and industrial and healthcare firms. They use the software to collect data from cars, jet engines, turbines, and even pacemakers.

Building a viable, secure platform is a huge opportunity. In June 2016, at the Viva Technology event in Paris, John Chambers, the executive chairman of Cisco, told a CNBC reporter that connected things could bring $19 trillion in economic benefits.

The holdback is still security. According to a December 2016 report from IBM Managed Security Services, cyber security attacks on control systems jumped 110 percent in 2016. Enterprises are having enough trouble keeping data secure on premises. They are reluctant to push computing out to the edge of the network where defenses are reduced.

Cisco believes the solution is blockchain.

The company is working with the Enterprise Ethereum Alliance to bring secure, smart contracts to the IoT. This might not seem like a big deal. It is revolutionary. An immutable ledger with smart contracts would eliminate the need for trusted intermediaries between communicating devices. It would also make it impossible for hackers to insert code and commandeer operational controls.

The applications, especially on the edge of the network, are endless.

Imagine tapping an iPhone to purchase a retail item. If both the iPhone and contactless payment system are connected to a blockchain, the transaction is completed only when each party can be independently verified through encryption. There is no opportunity for fraud.

Smart cars can communicate with traffic lights. Industrial robots can talk with other robots, and even schedule preventative maintenance.

Slock.it, a Swiss start-up, built an Ethereum blockchain application that lets owners and renters make secure transactions with no more than a smartphone application and a special connected lock. In theory, owners can securely rent, sell, or share anything without meeting the person on the other side of the transaction.

Cisco is helping enterprises build these kinds of applications.

The company has been plagued with flat revenues through the past five years. However, investors are beginning to see the growth potential for its new businesses. I believe that is wise. Connected devices and edge computing are a huge opportunity.

HOW TO PLAY: Cisco stock rallied 80 percent from 2016 through mid-2018, finally emerging from its demise in the aftermath of the dot-com bubble. It's a buy on pullbacks.

Fast Forward

Today, blockchain is a long way from its humble bitcoin roots. Software developers all over the world are working furiously to bring distributed ledger systems to banking, shipping, and even the growing refugee problem.

Blockchain seems to be a favored solution for most sectors plagued by middlemen and grifters. As a technology, there is tremendous promise. Developers see a rock solid system that is impenetrable for all of the reasons traditional systems are not. Blockchain decentralizes trust.

The anarchists see a way out from under. Bankers see reduced fees to third parties. There is something for everyone.

Microsoft and Cisco Systems are not exactly up-and-coming start-ups. At one time, each was the most valuable company in the world. Their roles in blockchain stem from noting the opportunity much earlier than their large brethren. Although blockchain is still young, there is something there. Microsoft and Cisco have established beachheads. The companies have become technology partners to the biggest syndicates. That is a strong competitive advantage.

CHAPTER 9

SELF-DRIVING CARS: THE ULTIMATE PARADIGM SHIFT

No emergent technology has captured more public interest than self-driving cars. We have been dreaming about driverless, electronically chauffeured vehicles since the interstate became a thing. Now they are close, really close. And they are going to change the way cars are sold, used, insured, and owned.

In this chapter, I will begin with a pair of frugal Carnegie Mellon engineers and end with the likely existential impact autonomous cars will have on the retail automotive business. In between, I will show how the development of artificial intelligence, sensors, and 5G networks has pushed the envelope. I will also provide a look at three unlikely winners as the world moves from smarter driver-assisted technologies to full autonomy.

The Road Trip

In 1995, Dean Pomerleau and Todd Jochem set out on a cross-country road trip. The Carnegie Mellon University Robotics Institute researchers wanted to prove that self-driving vehicles were possible.

With a shoestring budget of $20,000, they cobbled together off-the-shelf computer parts, a fiber-optic gyroscope, a GPS receiver, and a salvaged Pontiac minivan.

Their trip would take them from Pittsburgh to San Diego, a 2,849-mile journey.

At the time, public skepticism was high. The idea that a car could self-navigate seemed like science fiction. Even their colleagues had doubts.

In the end, their Pontiac Trans Sport completed 2,797 miles without driver input, about 92 percent of the trip.

By 2018, just 13 years later, autonomous vehicles are largely considered a solved problem. In between, there has been an exponential advance in the pace of information technology growth. From artificial intelligence, to better and cheaper sensors, to powerful cloud computing networks, all of the pieces have fallen into place.

And very soon we will have swift 5G wireless networks to accelerate the pace of development further.

Skeptics Have a Vested Interest

If you listen to the automotive industry, self-driving cars are still 15 years away. They would like for it to be so. The arrival of autonomous cars is going to change everything. It is going to be especially detrimental to the business of making and selling cars.

It will disrupt carmakers in the same way digital cameras upended Kodak. Units sold will fall off a cliff. When car ownership no longer makes economic sense, its 100-year-old business model will be turned completely inside out.

In a paper titled "Shared Autonomy," Morgan Stanley equity analyst Adam Jonas explains how the inevitable migration from the old business model to ride sharing and ride hailing will transform the car business into a highly regulated and intensely price-competitive utility. That will mean profound changes for the way cars are sold and insured. It will also disrupt airlines, energy, real estate, and utilities.

The reason is math. Traditionally, automakers have relied on simple metrics like units sold and average selling prices. In 2016, 80 million cars were sold at an average price of $19,000, for a total of $1.5 trillion in industry revenue.

The new Silicon Valley global mobility model places the emphasis on miles driven. Approximately 10 trillion miles were driven in 2016. The average cost per mile was $1, for a total of $10 trillion.

To get an idea of what this represents, Toyota runs the biggest car business in the world with sales of about $250 billion. Global mobility will be a business 40 times that size.

Carmakers and private-equity investors can do the math, too.

General Motors, Volkswagen, and Toyota have made major investments in mobility businesses. Toyota has placed its bet with Uber. In August 2017, the Silicon Valley super start-up announced it would begin testing a fully autonomous ride-hailing service in Pittsburgh.

Morgan Stanley analysts think autonomy is the tipping point. "We believe shared and autonomous cars can deflate the cost per mile to as little as 20 cents, triggering a doubling of global miles travelled by 2030," Jonas says.

At that cost, it no longer makes sense for consumers to buy vehicles. So, auto dealerships no longer make economic sense. The business-to-consumer auto insurance model collapses, given diminished risk. Ride hailing, especially for groups, becomes cost-competitive with short, regional air travel. Skipping the TSA lines is an added bonus.

Public parking spaces become mostly obsolete, yielding huge swaths of valuable urban real estate. And the economics of electric vehicles for fleets hastens the migration away from fossil fuels, leading to an energy glut and more heavily taxed electricity infrastructure.

Despite the disruption and considerable collateral damage, the new mobility business model is gaining momentum.

In 2015, there were 36,000 traffic deaths in the United States, or 100 per day. That was an 8 percent uptick from 2014. Ride hailing, later augmented with autonomy, is widely believed to be safer. President Obama announced guidelines for self-driving cars in September 2016. The Trump Administration has been receptive too. California reversed an earlier decision and will allow vehicles without steering wheels and brake pedals on public roads.

You get the point: Momentum is building.

"We see the greatest value in the content and data produced and consumed by the 68 million years of collective humanity trapped inside a mobile, supercomputing cyborg swarm. This precious time is ripe for liberation and monetization," Jonas writes.

Put in those terms, it is easy to see what is really happening. Self-driving cars are liberating. Ultimately, the gift they give consumers is not just improved safety alone. It's time.

I can't help but think of the louvered, silver-skinned DeLorean of the *Back to the Future* film trilogy, an iconic car that has a special place in the hearts of '80s culture fans. Bear with me, here.

While the technology to meet your high school mom or straighten out your grown kids still does not exist, the rise of autonomous vehicle technology is set to bring to market a "time machine" in a different way: a way to give nonproductive time back to consumers, just as the washing machine, microwave, telephone, and the Internet have in years past.

Jonas estimates that the technology could be worth 400 billion hours per year in saved time. At an average productive value to the economy of $10 per hour, that could add $4 trillion in new wealth per year.

Jonas and the Morgan Stanley analyst team made a few assumptions.

They pegged global vehicle miles traveled at around 10 trillion miles, or slightly less than 10,000 miles per unit on average for the slightly more than one billion cars on the road.

Average vehicle speed was set at 25 miles per hour, which is slightly less than the average speed of 32 mph in the United States as estimated by the US Department of Transportation. The *Wall Street Journal* reported that in 2014 the average speed in Beijing was 7.5 mph. Slow pokes.

The estimate of 400 billion hours excludes the time spent in vehicles by passengers. Average occupancy per vehicle in the United States is around 1.55.

The rest of the calculations get a little messier: estimating the value of an hour for the portion of the world fortunate enough to own automobiles individually and how much more folks who own cars make versus those that don't.

Still, it's incredible to think of the potential here. Instead of white-knuckling the steering wheel in traffic, millions will be able to sleep, work, shop, learn, watch films, or connect with family and friends instead. Not only will self-driving cars enable this, but the rise of ride-sharing services will as well.

The takeaway from all this is that with the concept of hands-free driving still in its infancy, we are only now beginning to understand the benefits, from lower insurance risk to fewer fatalities to more leisure time.

I realize now that many people say they love to drive, but in time we are going to realize that most people are not capable of being in charge of a two-ton vehicle hurtling down the freeway at 70 mph at night in the rain. Personal driving is a public safety hazard and will disappear. In its place will come more freedom.

HOW TO PLAY: If Morgan Stanley analysts are right, the best way to play this big trend is with leisure and hospitality stocks. **Netflix** (NFLX), **Facebook** (FB), and **Constellation Brands** (STZ), the fast-growing premium wine, spirits, and beer company, are attractive.

Deep Learning Speeds Cars Toward Their Destiny

In December 2017, *Wired* published a deep dive into self-driving cars with the title, "After Peak Hype, Self-Driving Cars Enter the Trough of Disillusionment." The author set up the straw man. Getting cars to drive autonomously with software and sensors is tremendously hard work.

Investors should understand that as the opportunity.

Most companies are not interested in hard work. In 2005, a fledgling Seattle online bookseller began building cloud-computing infrastructure so large it was capable of processing thousands of e-commerce transactions per second.

The very idea seemed implausible. It required massive data centers and new software processes. But Amazon.com did build Amazon Web Services, and its online store flourished.

Five years later, that same cloud network infrastructure became the foundation for the transformation of Netflix. It allowed programmers to build radical data-compression algorithms. They built new recommendation engines, too. In the process, a mail-order DVD rental company grew into a global streaming media behemoth.

Amazon and Netflix managers were successful because they saw that information technology was progressing at an exponential rate. They saw an opportunity to reimagine what was possible. They confounded the linear thinkers and created staggering shareholder value.

From 2009, the start of the current bull market, through mid-2018, Amazon shares were up 2,260 percent. Netflix shares were 6,320 percent higher. Those figures are not typos.

Self-driving car technology is being driven by the same escalating advances.

As mentioned a few moments ago, in 2010, Nvidia was a small company best known for high-end video graphic cards. Managers quickly realized that the same algorithms that allowed graphics designers to build simulated worlds in computer games could be used to solve more complex real-world problems.

Since then, the company has invested $10 billion in research and development. Self-driving cars ate up a sizeable chunk. By 2018, its Drive PX2 platform had become universally embraced by carmakers.

Huang, the Nvidia CEO, tells the story of betting the future of the graphics card company on AI because he could see the exponential growth ahead. Company engineers didn't accidentally build the best solutions for autonomous vehicles. It was foresight and a lot of hard work. Since 2010, its shares are up tenfold.

Yet, the scale of what Nvidia is doing may still be underappreciated.

The essence of Nvidia and its hold on the future of computing are based on artificially intelligent software. Long ago, the company committed to data science that allows computers to think, see, and learn like humans. Deep learning based on graphic processing units has been embraced by computer scientists. That exponential adoption by cutting-edge customers is driving Nvidia's bottom line.

In October 2016, Tesla showed off a self-driving vehicle equipped with Nvidia Drive PX hardware. The car successfully navigated busy residential streets, winding country roads, and the interstate before parallel parking in front of the corporate storefront. Daimler, Audi, and others are using Nvidia neural networks to advance their self-driving platforms, too.

In Germany, Deutsche Post DHL Group is set to begin a pilot program with fully autonomous delivery trucks in the fall of 2018.

These are real programs with real self-driving vehicles. They are not far-off concepts. They are here now.

And other fields are progressing at an exponential rate, as well. Faster networks will make detailed, real-time 3D maps a reality. At the same time, latency will be negated. Better radar and ultrasonic sensors are coming, too.

Again, the best way to play this trend is probably Nvidia. It is making the right connections, has best-in-class hardware and has the most potential in noncorrelated industries.

Cheaper, Smaller Sensors Usher in Self-Driving Cars

Most people just can't imagine the cumbersome robot cars we see in the media today will ever become good or cheap enough for widespread use.

A big hurdle is LiDAR, the light-based radar technology that autonomous cars use to see. Apart from looking like a KFC bucket, the rooftop sensor has been prohibitively expensive. Yet, a few years after introduction, prices are plummeting and new hardware is small enough to hide in body panels.

It is a remarkable development. It also brings self-driving cars closer than you think.

Rapid change is the common denominator of this era. The progression of information technology occurs so rapidly that things that seem impossible become reality. It's the age of invention—on steroids.

In January, Waymo, the autonomous vehicle subsidiary of Alphabet, announced its engineers managed to cut the cost of the LiDAR sensors used in its test vehicles by 90 percent. A two-unit system carried a $150,000 price tag as recently as 2012.

In early 2018, a Silicon Valley start-up called Luminar

made news with a new gallium arsenide LiDAR sensor capable of recognizing objects with low reflectivity up to 200 meters away. Austin Russell, its founder, began working on LiDAR technology before he could drive. Now he is claiming a breakthrough that may mean many young people never need a license.

Likewise, Velodyne announced a new, low-cost solid-state LiDAR system called Velarray. It boasts the same 200-meter range and improved vertical and horizontal fields of view and aims to sell for just a few hundred bucks when produced in mass volumes, according to a press release.

Velarray will work with both self-driving and ubiquitous Advanced Driver Assistance Systems such as adaptive cruise control. It is also small enough to fit in the palm of your hand.

All of that is important. Getting affordable LiDAR technology into the mainstream is a vital first step for self-driving cars. Once that happens, everything will change.

In 2015, Boston Consulting forecast the market for self-driving technologies may reach $42 billion by 2025. While that is a big number, it's still probably way too small. However, most important, it is big enough to get the ball rolling.

It is big enough to foster further development.

Why 5G Networks Will Be a Game Changer

Wireless networks 20 times faster are just around the corner.

In January 2018, **Qualcomm** (QCOM) announced a partnership with six leading Chinese smartphone manufacturers to begin rollout of 5G networks in 2019.

That would be years ahead of schedule. And the implications for investors are significant.

We are living in an era of exponential progress. Information technology is benefiting from the intersection of powerful cloud computing networks, big data analytics, and artificial intelligence.

Innovation that was science fiction a decade ago is not only possible, but investment opportunities are also developing right now.

And 5G stands out as a real game changer.

Next-generation networks promise data download speeds of 20 GB per second. Today's LTE networks, as great as they are, pull speeds of just 1 GB per second.

Liam Griffin, the CEO of **Skyworks Solutions** (SWKS), put the speed gains in perspective.

With 3G, it took about a day to download an HD movie, he told CNBC's Jim Cramer in 2017. LTE slashed the time to minutes. A 5G network would reduce the wait time to seconds.

That kind of speed changes everything. Latency would disappear. Engineers could build networks of connected vehicles that would relay relevant traffic information and automatically maintain safe driving distances. Telemedicine would become viable. Imagine a world where doctors in Boston use cutting-edge robotics to perform delicate surgeries in Mumbai. Drones and self-driving cars would be able to build real-time 3D maps to operate more efficiently.

The stakes are high.

"5G will be the backbone of our digital economies and societies worldwide," said Günther Oettinger, a European digital commissioner.

He's right. And for Europe, the situation has become desperate.

With Nokia and Ericsson, it was once the world leader in fast networks. Today, Europe's star is falling fast. Venture Beat reports that two-thirds of Koreans enjoy 4G. The United States and Japan have adoption rates at 45 percent and 42 percent, respectively. In Europe, the metric is just 10 percent.

In 2015, Europe started coordinating efforts with China. It has similar agreements with Japan and South Korea. The goal was to implement joint research, identify the most promising radio frequencies, and promote global standards.

The Qualcomm deal with Lenovo, Oppo, Vivo, Wingtech Technology, Xiaomi, and ZTE leaves the European Union on the outside, looking in.

The San Diego chip designer has been at the vanguard of 5G research. Now it has its stake planted in the heart of the most important wireless market in the world. In 2017, Counterpoint Research found that seven of the top 10 global 3G/4G smartphone manufacturers are Chinese.

Statista, an online research group, notes that there are currently 663 million Chinese smartphones in use. By 2022, that number is expected to grow to 817 million.

All of this means research and development of 5G applications will progress more quickly.

Qualcomm executives note that Chinese manufacturers are already making plans to use its 5G Pioneer initiative to build artificial intelligence and IoT applications.

That should be the key takeaway for investors. 5G is going to lead to next-generation applications and new business models. And it is going to happen quickly.

Self-driving cars is the first paradigm shift. It's not just about technology. It will radically change businesses like insurance, automotive parts, and leisure. It will also change many parts of the economy investors are not yet thinking about. It will lead to completely new enterprises and entire new business models.

Are You Ready to Rent Your Car?

There are 250 million cars in the United States. Most of them are sitting idle 23 hours per day. Increasing utilization would reduce pollution and congestion. It would also change the world.

Getaround, a peer-to-peer car-sharing service, is now one step closer to helping with that dilemma thanks to a $10 million investment from a Toyota unit called Mirai Creation. The money will help the start-up expand its peer-to-peer marketplace for on-demand car sharing in Chicago, Washington, D.C., San Francisco, and other cities. If that sounds familiar, think AirBnB, except for cars. Members rent out their own cars hourly, daily, or weekly based on rates they set. It's a great idea. There is just one catch. It's disruptive for companies that make cars.

Toyota executives see the writing on the wall, and they're staking a claim. In October 2016, the Japanese firm provided funding and a Mobility Service Platform and a smart-key box. It allows customers to unlock and start the shared car with no more than a smartphone.

Getaround founders Sam Zaid, Jessica Scorpio, and Elliot Kroo solved a big model problem way back in 2009. They approached a firm owned by Warren Buffett's Berkshire Hathaway (BRK.A) and came up with a bulletproof fleet insurance policy. Customers are prescreened for membership and insured for collision, comprehensive, and liability up to $1 million. The car owner's policy is not vulnerable.

The business opportunity for Getaround—whose app includes rental ads—is in line with many other disruptive businesses. It is using software to turn car ownership into a service. It takes a hefty 40 percent fee for getting the parties together, arranging the insurance, and collecting the money. It does all of this in a sleek smartphone app.

This mobility-as-a-service business model is not lost on carmakers. In addition to Getaround, Toyota is a strategic investor in Uber. **Avis Budget Group** (CAR) owns Zipcar, a ride-sharing business with more than one million members. And **General Motors** and Audi announced similar services for the San Francisco area this year.

What sets Getaround apart is the peer-to-peer nature of the business model. Although it did recently absorb 200 vehicles from San Francisco-based City CarShare, there is no other fleet. In fact, the corporate mission is to reduce overall car fleets through increased utilization. The company claims that more than 200,000 members and 25,000 car owners are willing to share their vehicles for a fee.

Getaround currently operates in only a few cities but its ambitions are national and beyond. In 2009, Zaid and Scorpio were challenged by Google founder, Larry Page, to build a business that could benefit one billion people in 10 years. They decided to change the world by eliminating car ownership.

"We see a true long-term shift in how consumers will access transportation in the future, moving away from ownership toward access," Zaid told *Entrepreneur* magazine in 2014. "We have an opportunity to help shape that future."

They're off to a slow but steady start, and should accelerate in the next couple of years.

HOW TO PLAY: As the world turns digital, the companies that enable mobile transactions become more important. The best way to play this trend in public companies is **PayPal Holdings Inc.** (PYPL) and **Square Inc.** (SQ), two up-and-coming digital payment firms.

Car Makers Want to Sell You a Subscription

Volvo is simplifying its powertrains. Now it wants to simplify the way it sells vehicles.

The iconic Swedish carmaker with the Chinese parent has a new plan to get millennials into its cars: subscriptions. Sort of like the way telecom carriers sell iPhones, except with cars.

It makes sense. And it's sweeping through the marketing world.

The root of Care by Volvo is reducing friction. The company will take care of the pesky stuff like insurance, maintenance, and repairs. Then customers can design their own packages around their individual needs.

Want a concierge service? Check. Refueling and cleaning? Check. Want to impress future in-laws next weekend with the new XC-90? You can do that, too.

There is even a service pack that includes a new upgrade every two years, naturally.

For its troubles, Volvo would get a monthly subscription fee that rises with the level and complexity of services selected. It's innovative. It's also entirely necessary. The corporate world is wrestling with how to market to a generation that would much rather spend income on restaurants and travel than durables.

Millennials were born into the sharing economy, and they like it.

They don't buy music or DVDs. There is a smartphone app for that. Spotify, the leading music-streaming service, now has 140 million active users. Fifty million pay a monthly fee.

They don't buy cars. There is an app for that, too. Uber, the leading ride-hailing company, operates in 84 countries and served two billion rides in 2016.

Brian Chesky, founder of Airbnb, a home-sharing company, put it best: "Access is becoming the new ownership . . . our bling isn't our house or our car, it is the theatre of Instagram and the experiences we are having in the world."

Care by Volvo is an attempt to bring the auto industry into the age of access.

It comes as the industry deals with declining sales, and the prospect of innovation, like self-driving technologies, may kill the ownership business model altogether. Car companies are getting ready.

BMW is trialing a ride-sharing service called ReachNow. General Motors bought an automated driving technology company, invested $500 million in Lyft, Uber's largest rival, and is starting its own car-sharing service. Companies from **Fiat Chrysler** (FCAU) to Ford (F), Volkswagen, and Mercedes have similar deals in the works.

It's a crazy, mixed-up time, fostered by changing societal values and emergent technology.

For investors, it does not have to be perilous. Opportunities abound. Companies are building vibrant new business models around access.

From 1995 through 2011, **Adobe Systems** (ADBE) had a vibrant shrink wrap software business. Adobe Illustrator and Photoshop were big-ticket software titles that quickly became the industry standard for creators. Then, the company moved the entire business online with a monthly subscription model. In 2018, the company was 10 times more valuable.

Apple is the world's largest company by market capitalization, at least through mid-2018. It logs the bulk of its sales through lucrative annual contracts with wireless carriers. In 2015, it began pushing its own upgrade program to people shopping online and at its stores. It turns out that selling subscriptions is easier than convincing them to buy an expensive new phone each year.

Volvo is hoping to catch some of that magic.

Self-Driving Tech for the Masses

In January 2018, Waymo showed off a driverless minivan.

It carefully navigated public streets as excited passengers watched from the backseat.

Investors should ignore the naysayers. Everything is about to change in profound new ways.

Still, don't expect a self-driving Chevy Malibu any time soon. Like most automotive innovations, the really cool stuff will land in high-end cars first.

After all, somebody has to foot the bill for research and development: like the buyers of Mercedes, Audis, Teslas, and Cadillacs.

However, the masses will soon be served by autonomous taxibots, trucks, and logistics vehicles. Engineers have been toiling with code and robotics for years. In the interim, the supporting technology has blossomed.

The Drive PX Pegasus, Nvidia's latest AI supercomputer, is

ready for full autonomy. And it fits inside a container the size of a lunchbox.

It's no wonder that taxi, trucking, and logistics companies are clamoring to get their hands on it.

In Singapore, nuTonomy, a Boston software company, is already ferrying passengers in fully automated taxibots.

In the United States, Daimler tested running digitally connected autonomous trucks in convoys on an Oregon highway.

These projects are in addition to the Deutsche Post DHL Group automated fleets planned for Germany in the fall of 2018.

All over the world, companies are working feverishly to bring autonomy to vehicles. The process has moved out of the labs and onto public streets. It's happening. It's real.

For investors, this is a sea change. It means old business models must be revamped. It also means so many new opportunities.

Over the long term, automakers must adapt to the likelihood of declining sales. In the near term, they must retool. Vehicle interiors will undergo radical changes.

Cars will become more like living rooms. They will be places where data, media, and even alcohol are consumed. Think about that for a moment. Think about the new growth vectors once "commuting cocktails" become a thing.

It will also change the supply chain.

The reason logistics companies are leading the charge toward autonomy is that the last mile is the most expensive part of their business.

Improving efficiency, even incrementally, goes straight to the bottom line. In a competitive, transparent corporate world, those savings will be passed on to customers. It will be a boon to retailers.

And it brings the prospect of self-driving cars full circle: As the use case for vehicles changes, it will have widespread effects on the business of selling cars. It is the reason automakers keep trying to put off the inevitable. It is the reason their spokespeople keep telling us how much we want to drive.

> **HOW TO PLAY:** One way to play fully autonomous cars is **Qualcomm**. The maker of wireless radio protocols will play a big role in 5G, a necessary development for the rollout of self-driving vehicles.

The Coming Crash in Car Sales

In my six decades of life on Earth, the most profound technology changes have been personal computing, digital networking, and the rise of mobile communications.

I suspect that one of the biggest technology changes coming for children born right now will be in energy and transportation, as solar power eclipses fossil fuels and the autonomous car eclipses personal driving.

Let's take a moment to consider changes coming to driveways, highways, and parking lots near you. I'm going to lean heavily on the research of Barclays analyst Brian Johnson as reported in *Bloomberg* recently.

The article by Keith Naughton, quoting the Barclays report, noted the following: US auto sales may drop about 40 percent in the next 25 years because of shared driverless cars, forcing mass-market producers such as General Motors Co. and Ford Motor Co. to slash output.

Vehicle ownership rates may fall by almost half as families move to having just one car. Driverless cars will travel twice as many miles as current autos because they will transport each family member during the day.

Large-volume automakers will need to shrink dramatically to survive. "GM and Ford would need to reduce North American production by up to 68 percent and 58 percent, respectively," Johnson wrote.

The market for autonomous technology will grow to $42 billion by 2025 and self-driving cars may account for a quarter of global auto sales by 2035, according to Boston Consulting Group. Partially autonomous cars will be available as soon as 2017.

When most vehicles are driverless, annual US auto sales will fall about 40 percent to 9.5 million, while the number of cars on American roads declines by 60 percent to fewer than 100 million.

"While extreme, a historical precedent exists," Johnson wrote. "Horses once filled the many roles that cars fill today, but as the automobile came along, the population of horses dropped sharply."

Four vehicle categories will emerge: Traditional cars and trucks driven by individuals for work or in rural areas; *family autonomous vehicles* owned by individuals and shared by a single family; *shared autonomous vehicles* that would be "robot taxis" summoned by smartphone; and *pooled shared autonomous vehicles* that accommodate multiple riders, like a bus or a van.

Every shared vehicle on the road would displace nine traditional autos, and each pooled shared vehicle would take the place of as many as 18, according to Johnson's report.

Consumers' cost of mobility would drop dramatically. By removing the driver from the equation, the average cost per mile to the consumer could be 44 cents for a private ride in a standard sedan and 8 cents for a shared ride in a two-seater. That would be well below the $3 to $3.50 a mile consumers now pay to ride in an UberX car or the $1 to $1.50 a mile for an UberPool vehicle.

The shift to driverless vehicles would benefit transportation network companies such as Uber Technologies Inc., autonomous technology providers such as Nvidia, and makers of low-cost vehicles.

"While the Detroit Big 3 will still have pickups and vans (their most profitable segments), they will be challenged in the markets for family autonomous vehicles and shared vehicles," Johnson wrote, adding: "We see this as a further lid on the prospects for traditional, mass-market automakers."

This is a really big deal and it's going to happen. Other organizations that will have to start preparing now for this future are parking lot owners; auto dealerships; auto insurers; auto finance companies; municipalities that depend on taxes from auto dealer rows; auto workers; mall owners who have devoted tens of thousands of acres to parking; and emergency rooms that deal with the results of thousands of auto accidents.

For investors, a sensible vehicle to take advantage of these developments, as mentioned before, is Nvidia. The graphics card maker transformed itself into an AI company back in 2010. Since that time, it bet early, and very well, on self-driving cars. Its shareholders have been very well rewarded already and will not be disappointed by the next phase of the industry's development. This story is only beginning.

Old-Line Car Parts Makers Get
in on the Action: Aptiv

Earlier this year, Delphi, an old school auto parts company, reorganized. Managers wanted investors to draw distinctions between its legacy auto parts businesses, and the forward-thinking Auto 2.0 franchises.

So, they spun off those assets into another stock with the old name.

The new stock, **Aptiv** (APTV), is a pure play on self-driving vehicles, ride-hailing, and autonomous technologies. This was a smart move on the company's part. That's because the technology is getting better at an exponential rate.

Also, managers have been working hard to build up those franchises.

In 2017, Delphi swallowed nuTonomy, a maker of self-driving software. At the time, it seemed like a desperate attempt by an aging company trying to stay relevant. It was a sign.

Delphi was not your father's car parts maker. It was a company making the transition to Aptiv.

The company was spun out for General Motors six years ago. Like any youngster with something to prove, the company promptly moved away, setting up shop in Britain. Since that time, managers have been making all of the right moves.

In 2015 they bought Ottomatika. The self-driving car software start-up was a recent spinout from Carnegie Mellon, a Pittsburgh school considered to be one of the premiere robotics engineering institutions in the world. The deal gave Delphi talent and intellectual property around self-driving cars.

It also gave managers the incentive to get bigger, faster. nuTonomy is the next logical step.

The Boston-based company made headlines last year when it announced it was putting a fleet of self-driving taxis on the streets of Singapore. As a company, nuTonomy raised $185 million. It even struck high-profile deals with ride sharing companies Lyft and Grab, and pushed its headcount to 100 engineers.

These developments played a role in the $450 million buyout.

The National Highway Traffic Safety Administration reports the number of traffic deaths surged to 37,000 in 2016. Despite safer cars, those grim numbers are on the rise. Drivers have become more distracted. Autonomous vehicles are safer, while providing accessibility and efficiencies.

Managers understood the stakes. They were also keenly aware that self-driving cars will not roll out to consumers immediately. Initially, the technology will be restricted to taxibots and logistics fleets operating on pre-mapped routes. The nuTonomy acquisition is a way to stay at the forefront of the technology.

Later, I expect Aptiv managers to leverage their extensive relationships with automakers to work software and parts deals.

That is the reason I'm bullish on the stock. The automotive sector is about relationships and long-term strategic planning. Aptiv is fully entrenched in the sector. Now the company has the latitude and the independence to pursue its ambitions as a key player in the autonomous car field.

This is a big opportunity. It will have lasting power as cars transition from more automated driver-assisted features to full-fledged autonomy.

Self-Driving Tech Will Transform Auto Suppliers

Aquantia (AQ) came public in November 2017. On paper, the company makes rather dull electronic components—integrated circuits for legacy Ethernet connectivity.

In the next era of autonomous vehicles, sensors, touchscreen monitors, electric motors, and onboard supercomputers will need multi-gigabit connectivity over copper connections. That is Aquantia's field of expertise.

The strength of the San Jose company is it found a way to make legacy hardware run five times faster, at lower power consumption.

Investors need to know what all of the fuss is about.

A legitimate connectivity revolution is underway. Network hardware upgrades and new standards have pushed wireless to blazing speeds. In many cases, downloads are faster on a smartphone with a good LTE connection than at the office. That is just bizarre.

Wired Ethernet standards have not changed since Google was birthed in a Stanford dorm room.

Since 2004, Aquantia has been searching for a new way forward. In 2014, the company launched the first 10 GB integrated circuit for data center servers. This design allowed multi-gigabyte throughput over standard copper circuits. In 2014, the company launched an enterprise version.

It quickly became the industry standard. Aquantia partnered with **Cisco Systems** (CSCO) and others to found the NBASE-T alliance, an advocacy group. Today the organization is 45 members strong. The baseline for the 802.3 bz standard was ratified by the Institute for Electrical and Electronic Engineers (IEEE) in 2016.

It is a big deal.

Faraj Aalaei, Aquantia's chief executive, says that more than a billion ports of Ethernet ship every year. Most of these handle east/west traffic. That is data moved over very short distances, usually between stacked servers. And while optical may be the longer-term future of data, that transition would require replacing the existing electrical infrastructure.

That is a jump many major network players are reluctant to make.

For example, Cisco and Intel, the leading maker of data center and client computing chipsets, have become Aquantia's biggest customers. And the business is growing, fast.

For fiscal 2017, total revenue was $103.4 million, up 19 percent. The full year net loss was $3 million.

There are some reasons for concern. Aquantia is still not profitable, Cisco and Intel comprise the bulk of sales, and there is the longer-term threat that optical will swallow that business whole, as data demands increase.

Aalaei claims that the future of the company is making high-speed multi-gig network chips for autonomous vehicles. AVs, with their constant connections and collection of sensors, are data centers on wheels. And Aquantia is gearing up with new products and partnerships. The company recently signed an agreement with Nvidia.

Long-term, the company appears to have a shot at being a winner. It has longstanding industry ties and the most likely technology bridge to self-driving cars. It's not flashy, but it is an important piece of the ecosystem.

Autonomous cars are coming; investors need to be on the curb, ready to go.

Fast Forward

Apple, Google, Intel, and even Domino's Pizza are all rolling along with autonomous vehicle research. All of the major automakers also have programs. It makes you think there is a real prize at the end of the chase, or that having no strategy is the road to ruin.

Most experts predict autonomous vehicles are coming in the next four years. New business models are on the horizon, too. Mobility-as-a-Service would finally get car utilization rates above 4 percent. Subscriptions also make sense. If smartphone makers can convince customers to upgrade $1,000 devices every two years, car companies should be able to do the same, especially if they fold in insurance and maintenance.

All of the change is the result of better sensors, software, and super-fast networks falling into place at the same time. Convergence is a big theme in the fast forward era.

HOW TO PLAY: Aptiv, Aquantia and, Constellation Brands are probably not the companies that first come to mind when you think about mind-bending new technology. That's fine. These companies appear to be in the right place at the right time. There is going to be a transition from the status quo to self-driving cars. Aptiv and Aquantia make some of the parts that car companies will need as that transition occurs. Constellation Brands makes the premium "commuter cocktails" that future riders will be sipping. And of course, as noted a couple of times, other top picks in the space are Nvidia and Qualcomm.

CHAPTER 10

THE INTERNET OF THINGS: SMART NETWORKS EVERYWHERE

The Internet of Things (IOT) is about technology convergence. In this chapter I will show how smart developers have used a combination of sensors, data analytics, and powerful cloud networks to make warehouse floors more efficient and households more accessible—and have even taken steps toward solving out-of-control healthcare costs. I will also discuss three IoT infrastructure companies that have secured a spot on the ground floor of this exciting new industry.

The Hive Mind

The "hive mind" is science fiction utopia. Keys are never lost, no fact unremembered, and no communications unsent. Imagine a state of total awareness.

Over the next 15 years, the IoT promises to connect every tangible item in the world and every person to immersive webs of dynamic intelligence. Your alarm clock will wake you early when traffic is slow, commercial aircraft will automatically schedule required maintenance, and misplaced personal items will alert you before you realize they're missing—and that is only the beginning of what is possible. Billions of connected devices continuously exchanging data will yield stunning productivity, environmental, medical, and human benefits, while also unearthing new security vulnerabilities.

It's one of the most lucrative investment opportunities of our lifetimes.

With changes so massive coming, you would think it would be easy to figure out how to take advantage. Most white papers at think tanks focus on the connectivity of the things, such as network equipment and sensors.

And to be sure, the recent spate of big semiconductor company mergers—i.e., Avago buying Broadcom, Intel buying Altera, and NXP Semiconductor buying Freescale—are aimed at scaling up to dominate the next phase of profound connectivity.

Yet most of the value of this brave new world will be in the software that compiles, analyzes, and instantaneously leverages the data collected by billions of sensors.

The IoT is a natural fit for General Electric, for instance. As the world's largest maker of jet engines, diesel trains, and other large industrial goods, finding ways to manufacture more efficiently is in its DNA. Developing a mesh of sensors and software was a logical step. So in 2013, GE unveiled a productivity software platform called Predix in conjunction with Amazon Web Services, Accenture, and EMC. The goal was to bring penny-pinching predictive data analytics to the industrial sector at scale.

Luckily, GE had a willing guinea pig for this project: itself. Since 2013, Predix has had a profound impact on GE's production lines. In 2015 it was able to save $500 million through predictive maintenance. And by 2020, the company is expecting savings of better than $1 billion as the software and sensors are connected to more machines.

Elsewhere, BMW and Ford expect connected cars will communicate with each other and the network, relaying key data points like speed and destination. Using that data the network will not only rout traffic and govern speed to relieve congestion, it will reduce accidents by constantly monitoring safe distances given weather and road conditions. In the nearer future, smart assist features like automatic braking will slow vehicles to avoid accidents even if the driver fails to reduce speed.

Johnson Controls (JCI) wants to take automation one step further with embedded sensors in roads, street lamps, traffic lights, buildings, and other infrastructure. It will collect, analyze, and make data useful, so lights and air-conditioning units shut off when nobody is around, traffic lights will change to moderate the flow of cars, and icy road conditions will be relayed to oncoming cars, alerting them to slow down. If the drivers blow off the information, the cars will automatically reduce speed.

Sensors alone are not enough; they merely collect data. When they are connected via software to empower real-time decision making, the magic begins.

IBM (IBM) is building a major presence in data analytics—particularly in healthcare—with its Watson computing platform. In 2015 the company launched the Watson Health Cloud. The idea was to build a secure, open platform in which corporations and researchers could build systems and exchange data using application program interfaces (APIs).

Already, pharmaceutical and medical device firms like **Johnson & Johnson** (JNJ) and **Medtronic** (MDT) are using it to develop new drugs. **Apple** (AAPL) and **Under Armour** (UA) are using Watson analytics to decipher the deluge of data from connected watches and fitness bands. And medical facilities like Memorial Sloan-Kettering Cancer Center have made Watson the centerpiece of oncology research.

The size of the potential market for IoT solutions could be huge. In 2015, research firm IDC predicted the total market would grow to $1.7 trillion in 2020, from just $655.8 billion in 2014. And the company is predicting a staggering 29.5 billion connected devices.

As the paradigm shift continues, many old business models will be upended, leading to new services, products, and industries.

Naysayers argue that IoT is only hype. They are wrong because their focus is the things, the machines. The power and promise is leveraging data. Sensors, machines, and real-time analytics mean we're entering an era when reaction times will be smaller than at any time in history.

Businesses will use smart networks to predict and remedy potential problems in real time. That state of total awareness is going to lead to unprecedented control over resources. In a business climate plagued with margin transparency and widespread disruption, this is more important than ever.

If All Else Fails, Blame Amazon.com

Back in 2012, Amazon.com bought Kiva, a robotics pioneer, for $775 million. At the time the company was building out warehouse infrastructure all over the world. The Kiva implementation was eye opening because its tiny motorized robots moved entire shelves. Very quickly, humans became the minority at the new state-of-the-art fulfillment centers. They were relegated to picking products from shelves whizzing by.

Now Amazon wants to replace the pickers too.

Every year, the company hosts the Amazon Picking Challenge. It is an international competition that honors engineering teams for building robots with human-like dexterity. In 2017, a Dutch robot with two fingers, a suction cup, and a network connection prevailed.

None of this plays well against the current political backdrop. Anxiety is high. Politicians on both sides of the political spectrum are looking for scapegoats. So they peddle a narrative steeped in gloom. The entire system is rigged. The forces of globalization are stealing jobs, destroying the future, they harangue.

The truth is that our economic system, capitalism, isn't predicated on providing jobs or bright futures for workers for that matter. Those things are happy by-products. Capitalists are supposed to disrupt and innovate, mostly by looking for efficiencies, ways to replace high-cost jobs with low-cost machines. On that count, according to most, they're about to really hit their stride. That may play even worse.

What Amazon.com did was digitize its business before digital became a thing. It invested in processes and machines that turned real-world analog events into data. Then managers added everything to their giant network and used the software to optimize.

The Kiva acquisition in 2012 was an inflection point.

The robotics company was building an ecosystem around its nifty little orange robots. Companies began to build software and hardware as layers. However, when Amazon scooped up Kiva, it decided to bring the whole operation in-house. Existing contracts were allowed to expire. Competitors were forced to scramble for new solutions.

Thankfully, they innovated. San Jose, Boston, and Europe are now full of automation start-ups anticipating the next wave of retooling. **Honeywell** (HON) bought Intelligrated in 2017 for $1.5 billion. Today these companies are stronger, smarter, and more agile. They're also ready to prune more humans than ever as they integrate drones and other logistics devices armed with artificial intelligence.

In fairness, Amazon has been a good corporate citizen. Founder Jeff Bezos talks with pride about Career Choice, a job training program started in 2012. The program allows warehouse workers to train for high-demand jobs beyond Amazon. The Seattle warehouse has a glass classroom visible to most parts of the site.

There, workers retrain for jobs in nursing, aircraft mechanics, and truck driving. This year Amazon is open-sourcing the program, encouraging other Fortune 1000 companies to do the same. Clearly, it's under no obligation to help workers find other or better jobs.

According to Bezos, this program exists so that workers can build careers in fields where demand is high and wages firm. He doesn't want workers to feel trapped at Amazon. Putting the classroom in a glass box on the edge of the warehouse floor sends a clear message: There are choices beyond the warehouse.

Automation and other productivity measures will take a toll on the rate and quality of employment in the future. While a quirky Dutch robot isn't likely to change the world, it does set the tone. Many future jobs in the IoT era belong to robots.

Businesses that network the things of the enterprise to inform decision making are likely to be rewarded with cost savings and productivity. It should not have come as a huge surprise. The process began long ago. Apple took a fledging digital media movement and gave it grace with iTunes. FedEx and United Parcel Service streamlined package delivery with digital waybill scans and automation.

However, Amazon.com took the best of both and put almost anything we could imagine just a few taps or clicks away with its giant online storefront. Bringing the physical warehouses inside the network was brilliant.

Now it is bringing predictability and unimaginable cost efficiency.

Walmart, Target, and GM Choose IoT

In 2017, the *Electronic Engineering Times* ran a story featuring Chris Enslin, a vice president at **Walmart** (WMT). His team of 500 is actively exploring ways to bring IoT, robotics, and artificial intelligence to the retailing giant's global network.

The idea that billions of connected sensors are going to change the face of commerce is not novel. Analysts and consultants have been predicting the emergence of IoT for several years.

In 2015, McKinsey, a global consulting firm, estimated the worldwide impact of smart systems could reach $11 trillion by 2025. The firm predicted enormous cost savings for healthcare due to preventative maintenance for general interopera-bility. There was a lot to like, with very little downside. Or so it seemed.

The holdup is sensors. They are still too expensive for wide adoption. Enslin admits IoT strategies remain immature at Walmart. Engineers have trials up and running at only a handful of its 12,000 stores. Even then, the applications are rudimentary.

They use heat and vibration sensors in refrigerators to increase food safety and provide preventative maintenance. Scanners and computer vision systems now read codes for packaged products, replacing legacy log management systems.

It's a start. And it's a baby step toward the next-generation end-to-end systems.

But at the right price, sensors could be attached to every product Walmart sells. "Intelligent packaging someday could help reorder products from home when they get low," Enslin says.

That would be valuable. And it is going to happen, sooner than later.

The company is locked in a fierce battle with **Amazon .com** for retail superiority. Although the online giant has only a fraction of Walmart's annual sales, it has leapfrogged the Arkansas company in market capitalization. Despite the often razor-thin margins at its core business, Amazon.com was early to adopt IoT. And it is exploiting its advantages.

We take distribution and e-commerce for granted, but the beauty of the model is loss elimination. Items are rigor-ously tracked throughout the supply chain, resulting in better inventory management. There is no need for seasonal sales to clear backroom stock. There is less shoplifting.

Walmart is not the only retailer investing in IoT strategies. In 2015, **Target** began the process of outfitting 100 stores with LED ceiling lights that track customers after they enter, then guide them to products by using their smartphones.

It is even stranger than it sounds. The system uses something called visible light communication (VLC). VLC uses the wavelengths in LED lighting. These flickering wavelengths are imperceptible to the human eye yet robust enough to encode product information and transmit that data to a smartphone camera.

Proponents say the system can pinpoint products and users far better than Bluetooth. VLC is being backed by Philips, GE, Acuity, Qualcomm, and PureLiFi, a Scottish start-up. The obvious benefit, in addition to low-cost LED lighting, is putting customers on the network, where the experience can be personalized, promotions might be tailored, and data tracked.

General Motors has big plans for its Lake Orion manufacturing plant, 30 miles north of Detroit. The plant is home to its Chevy Bolt. The electric vehicle is considered vital to the longer-term health of GM.

As plants go, Lake Orion is a gem. It has 800 modern robots in place. From welding to lifting and painting, the bright yellow machines are constantly twisting and buzzing. Partners **Rockwell Automation** (ROK), Cisco Systems, and Fanuc, the Japanese robotics manufacturer, have worked hard to wring out efficiencies.

In 2016, the Lake Orion plant got the ultimate upgrade. GM installed a "mother brain"—a software stack that connects all of the hardware and data. Plant managers say for the first time, robots, conveyor belts, and even the HVAC are being run with the same software centerpiece. That computing center is located in a cloud set up by Cisco, running custom algorithms developed by Fanuc. The result is predictable manufacturing bliss and big cost savings.

Alexa Will Pay Your Bills

Echo, the smart speaker developed by Amazon, is on a roll. Not long after Echo became the top choice for consumers looking to automate their home, and after two voice-activated companions were added, Amazon set up a clever collaboration that makes it more useful for financially conscious users.

Capital One Financial (COF) announced a new skill for Alexa Voice Search at SXSW in 2017. The tiny software hack allows enabled Amazon Echos, Taps, Echo Dots, and Fire TVs to interact with a person's financial information.

This helps bank customers stay on top of their credit card account by checking their balance, reviewing recent transactions, or making payments, as well as get real-time access to checking and savings account information, all hands-free.

Instead of using your computer, smartphone, or tablet to log into your online banking account or physically going to the bank, you can simply ask Alexa for the information.

To do this, users must first enable the Capital One skill in the Alexa app. After enabling the skill, users can ask questions such as:

- "Alexa, ask Capital One for my Quicksilver Card balance."
- "Alexa, ask Capital One for recent transactions on my checking account."
- "Alexa, ask Capital One to pay my credit card bill."

To avoid any confusion, Alexa will use pre-linked funds to pay bills. Though one would hope Alexa could use her own funds to pay your bills, that's not going to happen.

Though this latest IoT innovation from Capital One may demonstrate the company's commitment to creating better experiences, products, and tools for customers, one cannot help but wonder how secure this new connection is. Is it really wise to have a voice assistant blurt out your finances? Alexa, don't tell my wife I bought another fairway wood for my golf bag.

Automated Drones and Delivery Vans

In the future your package might be delivered by a drone, launched and tracked from a mobile data center.

That is not science fiction. It's what the next generation of IoT logistics looks like according to Daimler, which has reported a $562.7 million minority stake in Matternet, a Menlo Park drone start-up.

It will work with Mercedes-Benz Vans, a commercial vehicle unit building a new class of electric vehicles with fully automated robotic shelves, rooftop drone launch pads, and an onboard, intelligent cloud-based data network. The concept underscores how much software and data has disrupted traditional business models. As stuff becomes a service, manufacturers have just two choices: Move up the value chain or die.

Mortality is a great motivator. All over the globe, automakers are frantically buying up software companies or working strategic IoT alliances. Toyota invested in Uber, Volkswagen took an interest in Gett, and General Motors advanced ride-sharing firm Lyft $500 million to work together.

MB Vans division chief, Volker Mornhinweg, put it succinctly: "We are looking beyond the vehicle to the whole value chain and the entire environment of our clients."

Matternet is a good place to start. The company cut its teeth using rugged commercial drones to deliver medical supplies in the rough terrains and extreme climates of Haiti,

Bhutan, the Dominican Republic, and Papua New Guinea. In 2017 it began testing package delivery with Swiss Cargo and the Swiss Postal Service. This year it announced it would start a trial delivery service with the European logistics giant, DHL.

Daimler will integrate the drones with a new cloud-based logistics platform that is, at least in part, operated out of its vans. Onboard systems will automatically load the payload, swap spent batteries, and monitor the coordinates of deployed drones even when they are out of the line of sight. Daimler expects that drones will be capable of carrying packages up to 4.4 pounds and travel about 12 miles on a single charge. If a package requires a signature, there is no problem; the driver is along to handle the pesky details.

Drone usage for IoT logistics is clearly gaining traction. Amazon and Alphabet are pushing the Federal Aviation Authority to relax regulations to permit more commercial use in the United States. Qualcomm and AT&T recently announced a joint venture to use wireless spectrum to help drones navigate beyond the line of sight.

Daimler's investment is indicative of the promise for investors. Drones, cloud-based data centers, and IoT are converging.

Qualcomm is making a concerted effort to dominate the drone "system on a chip" market, integrating its mobile and IoT architectures.

Healthcare Makes the Connection

It was only a matter of time before companies started using powerful cloud-computing networks and connected devices to advance healthcare.

In 2017, Philips and Qualcomm announced a partnership to develop an important IoT healthcare ecosystem. Medicare estimates that $17 billion is spent each year on avoidable readmission costs. Frequently, the cause of readmission is patients suffering from the complications of multiple chronic conditions like diabetes. Qualcomm Life quietly developed the 2Net open device network and a suite of connected medication dispensers, biosensors, and self-care glucose meters. Philips Healthcare Suite is an open, cloud-based IoT platform for healthcare systems, providers, and individuals. The marriage of the two creates one massive, scalable ecosystem. It will also create a lucrative new healthcare sector, as providers move care from costly emergency rooms to the home.

PricewaterhouseCoopers suggests that the market for connected healthcare will grow to $61 billion by 2020. From current levels, that is an impressive growth rate of 33 percent annually. And all parts of the ecosystem are expected to prosper. Connected health devices should grow to $14 billion by 2020.

Connected services are expected to expand to $45 billion over the same time frame—from current levels that represent annual growth rates of 37 percent and 31 percent, respectively.

There is reason to believe the PWC numbers might be conservative. As healthcare costs rise at an unsustainable rate in most of the developed world, policymakers are reaching the broad consensus that maintaining health is just as important as treating conditions. Connected healthcare, especially for chronic sufferers, encourages patient self-management while at the same time reducing costs. It's a win-win.

The timing is right for Philips and Qualcomm too. Healthcare Suite has industry-leading core capabilities in data storage, data aggregation, and analytics. Advances in cloud computing mean all of this can be delivered at scale. And 2Net allows healthcare providers to build custom IoT applications for personalized treatment through the patient's medical device, smartphone, or, potentially, other wearable devices. It's not hard to imagine a world where a patient with an Apple Watch is in constant, real-time contact with software at his or her healthcare provider.

Philips' Jeroen Tas summarizes the prospects well: "Patient self-management combined with connectivity to a care network is an emerging model that enables scalable chronic disease management for patients and providers."

Connected Home Still a Work in Progress

At the 2017 Google I/O developer conference, the search giant unveiled its latest attempt to finally bring a Google version of the connected home to consumers.

The promise of the household IoT is massive. Truly smart, connected appliances we control by just talking are the stuff of "The Jetsons," the space age future we were all promised in the popular animated TV series. That explains the hype cycle and wild estimates from consultants and analysts who should know.

It also explains consumers' disappointment with various connected refrigerators and wine bottles that are just dumb.

Google has not helped. Its Android@Home platform debuted in 2012 and quickly failed. Despite plenty of arm twisting, Google couldn't get hardware manufacturers to adopt its standards.

The $3.2 billion acquisition of smart appliance maker Nest in 2014 also slipped into the standards quagmire. Even with the stewardship of Tony Fadell, the guy behind the iPod product development, Nest has disappointed.

Its woes with competing standards culminated in 2016 when it decided to brick devices running Revolv, an IoT platform it acquired to move its brand forward just a year previous.

With its new Home set of products, Google is taking a different approach. It's playing to our inner child delight and the surprising success of Amazon's Echo. Home is controlled by voice and leverages the things Google does really well.

Ask it to play music, a podcast, or even to watch something on your television and Home performs like a champ because it uses the protocols of the wildly popular Chromecast devices. Those same standards also allow the seamless coordination of multiple Home devices and connected speakers.

Ask a trivia question about the weather, a change on your calendar, or commute, and Home can do these things, too, because it's built on Google Search and your personal Google services. It knows you have a dentist appointment Thursday or that there's a traffic jam because of roadwork on your morning commute. You better leave earlier.

Home can also turn off the lights in Billy's room adjust the thermostat in the basement, and activate security cameras outside based on the standards Nest has nailed down.

That might be the only obvious near-term failing of Home. As a controller for the connected home, it's still reliant on Nest's progress. As a result, Google is taking a cautious approach with Home. Unlike Echo, that has become a free-for-all with developers, Google did not announce any open application program interfaces at its 2016 I/O developer conference.

The company says it wants to wait until it has a chance to iron out all of the little wrinkles that plagued its previous connected home offerings.

The lack of open APIs means developers won't be able to get Home to order Domino's pizzas or a Lyft ride share. And it may not work with appliances on competing platforms like Samsung's SmartThings. Google says it will eventually have open APIs—but it's behind.

That's not necessarily a terrible thing. It's still quite early in the connected home segment. Despite the promise of the IoT, many platforms are islands unto themselves.

In some ways it is understandable. Many companies, like Google and Samsung, want tighter control over the end product, especially the software. More open devices have found trouble. They have been easy prey for hackers. However, if the IoT is going to reach its true potential, better standards and wider adoption must emerge.

Black Hats Storm IoT Device Makers

In 2017, Bruce Schneier issued a wake-up call to the US Congress. Schneier is no Chicken Little. He's a noted security expert and public policy lecturer at the Harvard Kennedy School. He's also the chief technologist at an IBM security subsidiary. And he's worried.

The IoT is the most complex framework ever imagined. It also empowers attackers.

In October 2017, hackers took control of millions of connected devices using code made available on the dark web. They targeted Dyn, a service provider to many large websites. Their distributed denial of service attack shut down Amazon, PayPal, Twitter, and Spotify in many parts of America.

"Attacks scale. The Internet is a massive tool for making things more efficient. That's also true for attacking. The Internet allows attacks to scale to a degree that's impossible otherwise. [. . .] And this is more dangerous as our systems get more critical," Schneier said. "The Dyn attack was benign. A couple of websites went down. The IoT affects the world in a direct and physical manner: cars, appliances, thermostats, airplanes. There's real risk to life and property. There's real catastrophic risk."

It is the rest of the connected world that worries Schneier. The IoT is only as strong as the weakest link, and there is no incentive for smaller companies making inexpensive devices to invest in security.

"These devices are a lower price margin, they're offshore, there's no teams," he said. And a lot of them cannot be patched. Those DVRs are going to be vulnerable until someone throws them away. And that takes a while."

The prescription, according to Schneier is not something many in Silicon Valley are going to like: Regulation. He sees the need for government to step in and make sure connected devices meet minimum standards.

It is a sentiment echoed by Brian Krebs, a veteran cyber security expert. In September 2016, KrebsOnSecurity.com was the target of an unprecedented cyber attack.

In the parlance of Red Bull–guzzling hackers, it was standard "distributed denial of service": Throw so much junk data at a site that it cannot perform its intended service. It happens all of the time.

This attack was game changing because it probably wasn't the work of a nefarious nation state. It was very likely ragtag hackers using an arsenal of IoT appliances. Like TV's Mac-Gyver, they banded together scads of routers, IP security cameras, and digital video recorders, used software to make them compliant, then pointed every last one of them at Krebs.

IoT security has been a pressure point among researchers for a while. In an effort to keep costs low and the learning curve lower for neophyte consumers, manufacturers have rushed connected things to the market. Many have generic firmware and, worse, default passwords.

Creepy hackers have easily commandeered everything from home security cameras to baby monitors. The jump to using connected devices as weaponry was just a matter of time.

As an investigative journalist, Brian Krebs is no stranger to attacks. He made it his business to ferret out malware and expose cyber criminals. His work is so well regarded that Akamai provided DDoS protection to his own site *pro bono* before the attacks last year made that too costly.

The site has since been embraced by Project Shield, an Alphabet service that protects journalists worldwide and their right to free speech.

Last year Krebs published a long blog post exposing the inner workings of a hacked, online booter service called vDOS. That service brazenly sold DDoS exploits to would be cyber extortionists on a subscription basis. For as little as $30 per month, customers got exploits capable of taking most sites down.

Krebs alleges the hacker-for-hire operation helped coordinate 150,000 exploits, yielded $600,000 in bitcoin for site administrators over a two-year period, and was responsible for the majority of DDoS shutdowns worldwide during that time.

Further investigation led him through thousands of paying clients, their targets, and the masterminds to two Israeli teens, Itay Huri and Yarden Bidani. The pair was later arrested by the FBI.

Taking down KrebsOnSecurity was just payback from miffed cyber criminals.

More worrisome is the scale of attacks now possible using security-challenged IoT devices. More than 620 gigabits per second was blasted at KrebsOnSecurity. For the sake of comparison, in 2013 a DDoS exploit shot 300 gigabits per second at Spamhaus, an international organization founded to track e-mail spammers, and some said it threated the very Internet itself.

In a recent post Krebs said, "The idea that tools that used to be exclusively in the hands of nation states are now in the hands of individual actors, it's kind of like the specter of a James Bond movie."

In the Bond films, despite villain superpowers, the forces of good always win. Then again, there is usually just one villain, and they can't rent superpowers for just $30 a month.

> **HOW TO PLAY:** A good way to play IoT in a deliberate, long-term way is **Cisco Systems** (CSCO). The giant maker of network gear has a dominant position in the industry, and security has become an obsession of its new executive team. There are a lot of more focused players, but none with the scale of Cisco.

Building Through Example: Rockwell Automation

Rockwell Automation (ROK) is a strange story. It is the world's largest company solely dedicated to industrial automation. And it has been in this business since 1901.

A decade ago, however, Rockwell was broken. The Milwaukee conglomerate had grown big and unwieldy. Its plants, scattered all over the globe, didn't use the same information technology systems. They barely communicated.

In 2007, the company sold its Power Systems division to Baldor Electric Company for $1.8 billion. Company managers began to look inward. They wanted to practice what company sales representatives were preaching to the corporate world.

In 2008, the Rockwell introduced the Connected Enterprise, its plan to connect every facet of modern businesses. And the process began with its own sprawling operations.

At the time, the company had expanded to 20 global manufacturing facilities, with 22,500 employees and 400,000 stock keeping units (SKUs). Plant managers had been given wide authority. The result was many different manufacturing processes, enterprise resource planning systems, and chaos.

The goal was to bring everything under one umbrella. The overarching theme was connectedness.

The Connected Enterprise began by merging operational technology, like barcode readers, automated conveyors, scanners, and plant floor touchscreens, with the information technology systems. This required a full reworking of the corporate network, data analytics, and the disparate ERP systems.

In 2012, the company ditched its network structure in favor of EtherNet/IP, an open network infrastructure. A standardized enterprise resource planning system across all facilities followed. In 2013, the company rolled out Manufacturing Execution System, a set of processes that standardized workflows.

Backend, cloud-based software stitched everything together. By late 2013, Rockwell managers in Milwaukee could see live data at every plant. They could peruse quality reports and gauge productivity.

Every scanner, sensor, and barcode reader across the enterprise was connected to a signal live feed.

The results were stunning. It was a total restructuring of the supply chain. Inventory declined from 120 days to

79. Product quality increased 50 percent. On-time deliveries surged from the middle 80 percent range to 96 percent. Capital expenditures declined by 30 percent. And productivity increased 4–5 percent.

It's a great story to tell clients. It's the power of a comprehensive IoT strategy.

In 2018, there are plenty of corporate managers willing to listen. They understand that IoT implementation provides benefits beyond simple productivity.

Rockwell claims an 82 percent success rate with IoT clients, with faster time to market, greater worker safety, improved network security, and lower total cost of ownership. In a highly competitive market where every advantage is magnified, these factors are vital.

The story is resonating with customers. In 2017, sales were up 7.2 percent to 6.3 billion year over year. And the company continues to grow very strongly in China, the United States, Europe, the Middle East, and Africa. These are key markets for IoT technologies.

In a conference call with analysts January 2018, Blake Moret, chief executive officer, stressed that the next corporate priority was strategic acquisitions to build out the connected enterprise strategy. He also congratulated managers at the Rockwell plant in Twinsburg, Ohio. The facility was awarded in 2017 for its use of innovative technology by *Plant Engineering* magazine.

HOW TO PLAY: Rockwell shares have performed very well since bottoming in 2008. The 10-year average rate of return is 12.2 percent. This has been a favorite for a long time. It is buyable into weakness.

> I have recommended the stock for years because company managers have had the vision and the commitment to be a big player in connected things. Given the potential size of this market, even at an $22.8 billion valuation in mid-2018, the stock is still cheap.
>
> The outlook for IoT spending is strong, and Rockwell is a proven performer.

Big Is Better: SAP

Sprawling. That is the best way to describe **SAP SE** (SAP).

The German enterprise software and professional services company has 345,000 customers and 87,000 employees, and its developers build solutions for 25 industries.

The company has the scale and expertise to win the IoT revolution. Investors should bet it will.

The company began in 1972 when a group of talented engineers left IBM. They wanted to move beyond math problems. They wanted to build deep relationships with customers. They wanted to run open, scalable software. What came next was R/3, the first standard application for real-time data processing.

It started a revolution.

In the early years, SAP routinely grew annual revenues by 60 percent. The company's software became a platform, allowing it to strengthen and grow inside enterprises. Engineers saw opportunities firsthand. When the Internet emerged in the 1990s, SAP was there to capitalize with new solutions. When e-commerce and social media followed, SAP augmented its platform further. And now the company is ready for next-generation IoT technologies.

Its SAP HANA is a big data platform that allows friction-less, fast analysis of data on any screen. From **Adobe Systems** (ABDE) to Mercedes Benz, leading companies choose the platform to rescue mission-critical insights swimming in a turbulent sea of data. Recent converts include **Nvidia** (NVDA) and China International Containers, one of the biggest makers of shipping containers in the world.

Speaking of containers, SAP is working with the shipping industry to build real-time solutions based on blockchain. Currently, international freight is a maze of middlemen. Bankers, insurers, carriers, freight-forwarders, and local authorities are all shifting paper between buyers and sellers. It is a mess.

SAP hopes to remedy this with a cloud-based solution that uses QR codes, two-factor authentication, and a distributed ledger system. Documents would be continuously updated and shared electronically. Bills of lading would be digitally signed by using mobile applications.

Plenty of companies are working on blockchain solutions. Very few have the scale and expertise to get inside enterprise boardrooms.

In 2018, SAP is getting into those boardrooms because corporate managers are anxious to use its software tools for IoT implementations. The power of HANA is its flexibility. SAP developers are using it to build real-time, next-generation IoT applications that are location aware and ready for machine-to-machine interaction.

The impressive sales growth is proof customers are voting with their wallets.

In 2017, SAP boasted $22 billion in sales. Despite its size, revenues were up 6 percent. Its cloud business is growing even faster. Luka Mucic, the CFO, told analysts in October that cloud licenses increased 15 percent year over year. Bookings were 19 percent better, and revenues jumped 27 percent.

But that is not the reason to buy SAP shares. The company is attractive because it is building a competitive advantage in IoT, a fast-growing industry vertical with tremendous long-term potential.

> **HOW TO PLAY:** SAP shares are a buy on pullbacks for long-term appreciation due to its IoT expertise and relentless innovation.

Connecting Things in the Cloud: Cloudera

Cloudera (CLDR) makes software that allows businesses to collect, store, and make sense of vast amounts of IoT data in real time.

The timing is right. Enterprises are on the edge of the IoT data deluge. They need firms like Cloudera to manage data and help drive insights.

The IoT is expected to connect up to 50 billion things to the Internet in a decade, says Amr Awadallah, Cloudera cofounder and chief technology officer. Sensors in smart cars, oil rigs, electric turbines, and everything in between will push a tenfold increase in the amount of data created over just the next four years.

Built on open-source Apache Hadoop, Cloudera's platform is capable of collecting and storing data across many sources in varied formats. And its roots in Yahoo and Google research labs mean it runs lean and seamlessly on hardware that is very low cost.

It can be a winning combination.

Truck maker Navistar runs its OnCommand diagnostics platform atop Cloudera Enterprise. Using weather, traffic, real-time vehicle performance, historical warranty, and other data, Navistar is able to predict maintenance issues before they occur. Vehicle downtime has been reduced by 40 percent, and the company is now able to remotely monitor 250,000 trucks.

Collecting and analyzing so many data points, across such a large install base, was simply "not possible" in the past, said Terry Kline, chief information officer at Navistar.

Opower uses Cloudera Big Data analytics to power its consumer-facing dashboard. The Virginia-based company works with utilities companies to help educate consumers about reducing their power consumption to save money. The software has resulted in $500 million in savings and three fewer terawatts of energy use. That's enough power to light up Salt Lake City and St. Louis for an entire year.

There are challenges. Founded in 2008, Cloudera was among the very first start-ups valued at more than $1 billion by the venture capital community. Accel Partners, Greylock Partners, Fidelity Investments, T. Rowe Price, and Intel all ponied up early funding in anticipation of a triumphant IPO. However, the company struggled with its business model. The IPO payday never came.

When you add in research and development, sales and marketing, and general administrative expenses, Cloudera is still losing money. The red ink was $187 million in fiscal 2017. That's down slightly from $203 million in 2016.

Awadallah believes the coming avalanche of data is the opportunity. Cloudera products are ready to be deployed across healthcare, insurance, manufacturing, financial services, and government.

In June 2017, he told Dataquest the sole purpose of Cloudera is to help customers maximize what big data can do for them. If he can deliver, big data is also going to be profoundly positive for Cloudera shareholders.

In April 2018, Cloudera reported that fourth-quarter revenue increased 42 percent year over year. Subscription revenue surged 50 percent to $84.3 million. In the first quarter as a public company, Cloudera introduced six new products and completed a major acquisition.

HOW TO PLAY: This is the early innings of IoT and big data. Cloudera stock holds tremendous promise because, despite its uninspiring 2017 IPO, it is the leading open-source provider in the space. Sooner or later, the industry will move toward open standards. Cloudera will be there to reap the rewards. It's not a buy right now, but it's one to put on your radar.

Fast Forward

The IoT gets a lot of bad press because it doesn't seem to be happening widely enough, fast enough. That will change, and soon. For most people, connected things are smart speakers and gadgets that were gifted during the holidays. We can see the potential, although only barely. Investors need to look past the things, and start thinking about the potential of leveraging data. There is a real IoT revolution happening on factory and warehouse floors, in supply chains, and during the last mile of logistics. Developers are using sensors, software, and supercomputer processing power to build perfect states of awareness. They are decreasing down time and doing preventative maintenance to increase productivity. And they are building systems that help patients decrease the chance of repeat visits to the hospital.

The IoT is a big investment trend in the making. Soon it will surround you, like the air. Just like a fish probably doesn't realize it is swimming, the lives of most people will be fundamentally transformed by IoT without their explicit knowledge. But that's fine; companies will still see the rewards and reap the credit.

CHAPTER 11

GENE EDITING: RESHUFFLING THE BUILDING BLOCKS OF LIFE

The Human Genome Project was a really big deal. Gene editing is too, but exponentially so. In this chapter I will show you how scientists have been able to build on their understanding of the human genome to carefully snip and edit DNA to grow more hearty food and fix crops that have been stripped of nutrients by higher levels of CO_2. I will explore pharming, the idea of modifying animal DNA to grow proteins for human medicines. And I will even show you how some scientists are skipping humans altogether and going straight to synthetic biology. They are creating DNA out of thin air. Finally, I'll delve into the business models of a couple of smaller companies that specialize in gene editing. Their shares are not for the faint of heart, but the potential is amazing.

In 2012, two biologists discovered that some genes naturally deploy an enzyme that prevents select DNA from attacking viruses. They learned that this enzyme can be used to precisely cut out specific genes in many scenarios. They called this CRISPR-Cas9, aka gene editing.

Questions about the ethics of creating designer babies aside, the discovery means it's possible to cut away bad genes in the human genome to cure diseases. However, for now the real potential is in hacking food. Researchers could use this technique to produce more hearty fruits, vegetables, and grains. They might even engineer disease-resistant livestock. And, at least in theory, all of these would be safe because no foreign genes are being introduced. Researchers are merely speeding up evolution.

Labor of Love: Writing New Human DNA

It really is a brave new world. Not long ago, a group of prominent scientists announced plans for a project to create synthetic human DNA from scratch.

That seems appropriate for Valentine's Day. If you don't like your lover, one day you might just be able to design a new one.

The project will be led by synthetic biologists Jef Boeke, of the Langone Medical Center at New York University, and George Church, of Harvard Medical School. And it will take up where the previous project to read the human genome ended.

You may recall that in 2003, the Human Genome Project (HGP) was completed. It was supposed to open the door to countless new treatments and cures for illnesses that had plagued humans for centuries. It didn't quite work out that way. It seems that understanding the relationship between genes and illness is more complex than scientists originally thought.

The new Human Genome Project-write, as the name implies, will attempt to synthetically write human DNA code. The idea is that writing and understanding genetic code made from scratch will help scientists learn more about those complex gene relationships.

And while creating the building blocks for human life in a lab may seem like science fiction, there is some precedent.

In 2010, scientists at the J. Craig Venter Institute created bacteria controlled by a synthetic genome, effectively turning code back into life. HGP-write will be like that experiment, only on a much bigger scale.

Writing DNA is tedious and expensive work. It involves precisely manipulating tiny amounts of chemicals and a DNA molecule.

These chemicals are sugar-building blocks designated A, T, C, and G, and they must be added in the correct amounts and the proper order hundreds of times to change the structure of DNA.

Boeke and Church believe completing HGP-write will shrink development costs for DNA fabrication by a factor of one thousand. If true, that could actually lead to all of the revolutionary treatments promised by the original Human Genome Project. Yet, pesky ethical questions remain.

These are heightened by Church's own colorful and controversial history.

According to Church, humans could be made immune to all viruses simply by removing the host material from our genes that viruses need to replicate. And that's just a start. He's been vocal about his efforts to resurrect the wooly mammoth now that perfectly preserved DNA material from the prehistoric beast has been recovered. Church is also using CRISPR, a gene-editing tool he helped develop, to alter pig genes so that their organs can be transplanted into humans. As for humans, he's not shy about his cradle-to-grave outlook.

He is aggressively in favor of gene editing to avoid potential birth defects, and he's working with gene therapies to reverse the aging process. It doesn't help that when he's pressed about ethics, he demurs to comparisons to the industrial revolution. This type of talk often lands scientists in hot water. And Church has been cooked so many times that he should have developed a rubbery exterior by now. He'll need it.

It could take at least $100 million and ten years to create the human genome from scratch. If the project is successful, scientists say they will restrict potential use cases to the petri dish to avoid ethical considerations. That's not exactly Mary Shelley's *Frankenstein*, but it is one giant step closer to Aldous Huxley's *Brave New World*.

HOW TO PLAY: As is often the case in biotech, the most reliable investment for investors in this space will be the proverbial picks and shovels: the makers of lab equipment and disposables, like **Becton Dickinson and Co.** (BDX), **Teleflex** Inc. (TFX), and **Cantel Medical Corp.** (CMD).

Transgenic Animals Hit the Pharm

Pharming is the concept of modifying animal DNA to produce human proteins for medicine. It's not just a catchy name.

Recent breakthroughs in gene editing mean it's going mainstream.

In December 2016, *The Verge* reported that Iowa Holsteins are being genetically engineered for their blood. This is not normal blood. It's as distinctive as their black-and-white coloring. SAB Biotherapeutics engineered it to be rich in human antibodies and proteins needed to fight pathogens like influenza, Ebola, or Zika. Pharming, or transgenic animals, is a big deal. It makes sense for a number of reasons.

Animal husbandry has been around for thousands of years. Hearty, more productive livestock are more valuable. Pharming is the logical evolution. Scientists use advanced biotechnology to splice in new DNA from another species. Typically, the transgenic animal will secrete valuable antibodies in its milk, eggs, or blood. From there, scientists just need to purify the proteins before using them to develop drugs for human use.

"I expect that we will see this progressing at light speed now," William Muir, a professor of animal sciences at Purdue University, told *The Verge*. "We know the technology, we know how to use it, and we're just waiting for, how many applications can we use it for?"

In the past, scientists used pigs and cows to produce insulin. By 1978, drug giant **Genentech** used biotechnology to make the synthetic version. Now biotechnology is facilitating the emergence of transgenic animals. Gene editing, using CRISPR-Cas9, is more accurate while also slashing costs.

And, some coveted proteins can be easily obtained by modifying the cell structure of mammals like rabbits, cows, goats, and sheep. Not only do animals produce significantly more proteins than other methods; in many cases, harvesting is no more difficult or invasive than collecting milk from a farm animal.

In 2009, **GTC Biotherapeutics** was granted FDA approval for an anti-clotting protein called antithrombin. The Framingham, Massachusetts, company produced the human antibody from the milk of 200 local bioengineered sheep. The *New York Times* reported that a single sheep produced as much antithrombin as 90,000 human blood donations.

In the case of SAB's Holsteins, 30 to 60 liters of plasma are being produced per month, per cow. This compares to just four liters per person, so you can see what an advance that is.

Moreover, *The Verge* reported that SAB's cows make polyclonal antibodies that "can attack bacteria, viruses, and even cancer cells in multiple areas."

While SAB's work is still in the FDA trial stage, it's clear recent advancements in biotechnologies are pushing developers toward transgenic animals.

Gene Editing Offers a Taste of Change

In the near future, scientists will engineer food that grows faster and does not spoil.

This is another promise of CRISPR-Cas 9, which is seen as a game-changing gene-editing tool.

Bioengineered food could significantly reduce world hunger. And, at least in theory, it would be perfectly safe.

It's all possible in this era of exponential progression in information technology.

Advances in compute power and data analytics led to the full reading of the human genome in 2003. Ever since, scientists have been building on the seminal event.

In the 1980s, scientists discovered how some bacteria used gene editing to defend against viral DNA. The bacteria used special enzymes to cut, copy, and store bits of viral DNA for future reference.

Twenty years later, researchers determined that the DNA of any organism could be snipped. By 2012, biologists Jennifer Doudna and Emmanuelle Charpentier demonstrated how CRISPR could precisely edit an organism's genome.

It changed everything.

With CRISPR, scientists can literally edit organisms, removing the bits that lead to unfavorable outcomes.

Ethicists worry about a rush toward designer babies. And there have been disturbing developments on that subject in China. However, the real opportunity in the near term has always been agriculture.

Organisms are constantly undergoing this process naturally. They evolve. It just takes time. Gene editing speeds the process, shaving off years, decades, and even millennia.

This is very different from GMOs, or genetically modified organisms. GMOs introduce foreign organisms to improve outcomes. Think of the end product as a Frankenstein.

For example, in 1994 scrappy young biotech Calgene won approval to sell the Flavr Savr tomato. To make a Flavr Savr, scientists genetically modified a garden-variety tomato with aminoglycoside 3-phosphotransferase II, a compound that kept the fruit from rotting.

The tinkering sabotaged the process that makes tomatoes turn squishy. But the less-squishy tomatoes never did catch on with a skeptical public. The company was later sold to Monsanto.

Speaking to *Wired*, Jennifer Doudna noted that CRISPR has the potential to speed up new crop development by several orders of magnitude.

In May 2016, scientists at Cold Harbor Laboratory in

New York published a report showing how gene editing might finally solve the pesky tomato problem.

Wild tomato plants drop their fruit. When the fruit hits the ground, it gets bruised or worse. So farmers harvest tomatoes early to prevent damage.

Then, to facilitate mechanical pickers, breeders played with the tomato plant's root structure. They wanted the fruit to hang on the branches longer. But nature got in the way. The new plants produced so many branches that harvesting became harder and yields actually declined.

The Cold Harbor researchers found the gene responsible for weird branches and edited it away.

They created a new tomato plant without extra branches that does not drop the fruit.

In 2015, Penn State researchers used CRISPR to remove the gene that caused white button mushrooms to discolor over time. Digital Trends reports that the group asked government regulators if the mushrooms fell under their purview. They did not. The mushrooms could legally go to market.

It's not surprising that Monsanto and Dupont, two of the industry heavyweights, have been enthusiastic early supporters of gene editing. It's cheaper and faster and does not suffer the stigma of transgenic modification. It's also safer.

Products are coming to market soon.

Gene editing is a game-changing technology that is emerging quickly. It would have been impossible two decades ago. Now it is on the near horizon. It will create many new business models. It will create new companies and sectors.

And don't assume the spoils will be limited to agricultural giants. This will impact equipment makers, landowners, and software developers. The implications are many.

A good way to start from the ag perspective is with major

crops giants like **Archer Daniels Midland** (ADM) and Calavo Growers (CVGW).

Blunting the Spread of "Junk Crops"

Your parents probably told you to eat your vegetables, so you could grow up strong and healthy.

Well, if you give the same advice to your children and grandchildren, you might be wasting your time.

That's because our farms are turning into fields of junk food.

Cutting-edge research indicates that fruits and vegetables may become less nutritious as carbon dioxide (CO_2) levels rise in the atmosphere.

Higher CO_2 levels in the air strip our crops of key micronutrients that we need to survive, according to Helena Bottemiller Evich, writing in *Politico*, September 2017.

And that is an opportunity for investors.

It is not supposed to be this way. Sunlight gives plants the energy to create food from water and CO_2. The process is called photosynthesis.

Higher CO_2 levels increase photosynthesis. And you'd think that would help plants grow faster and healthier.

Yet something's wrong. Plants are packing in more carbohydrates, which squeezes out proteins and key minerals like iron and zinc.

The result is fields of junk food.

It's a concept Irakli Loladze first learned in 1998 as a PhD student in Arizona.

The primary food of zooplankton is algae. Scientists were

able to dramatically increase algae growth with light. The result was an abundance of food for the microscopic sea creatures.

But the zooplankton were still starving. While plentiful, the algae lacked the nutrients that could keep the hungry microorganisms alive.

Loladze, now a math professor at Bryan College in Lincoln, Nebraska, has spent the past two decades researching these rising CO_2 levels and their impacts on plant life.

His view is apocalyptic. He told Politico: "We are witnessing the greatest injection of carbohydrates into the biosphere in human history."

Lewis Ziska, a plant biologist, spends most of his day studying the nutritional effects of plant breeding for the US Department of Agriculture.

As a wildflower, goldenrod has not changed much in 175 years. Its pollen is an important source of protein for bees.

But Ziska found that the protein content has been in steady decline since the Industrial Revolution. And bee populations are dwindling in lockstep. That's because bees can't survive if they don't consume enough protein.

These discoveries indicate that overdosing the Earth on CO_2 could deliver a fatal double-whammy to the human race.

First, humans could literally starve from eating food that has little nutritional value. Second, bees could go extinct—and our crops could die off without bees to pollinate them.

This is really bad news that has not penetrated the mass media. It has been the subject of TED talks and a fair bit of hysteria in smaller publications. Some argue that bees pollinate a third of the global food supply.

For investors, the fact that this is happening in an era of invention makes this an opportunity.

The exponential progression of information technology, coupled with abundant capital and entrepreneurship, means anything is possible.

Add that to today's ubiquitous, affordable access to super-computers—plus advances in data analytics and modeling—and you have a recipe for new-level problem solving.

Biotechnology companies are already on the case using CRISPR-Cas9.

The gene-editing technique allows scientists to precisely edit an organism's DNA, removing the bits that lead to unfavorable outcomes. As mentioned a moment ago, this technology can even let scientists build life from scratch.

Agricultural technology companies are in the mix, too. Tractors use sophisticated tracking and self-driving systems. They have sensors to identify either pesky weeds or crops that need more water.

And everything is being networked so data can be crunched and methods perfected.

It's hard enough to sustain momentum on discussions about climate change, let alone begin discussion about what CO_2 is doing to the food we eat. Yet, there is a growing body of evidence that our food supply is in peril. Fortunately, scientists are creating the tools to blunt the danger.

Biologist Ready to Build Life from Scratch

George Church, the Harvard geneticist, is one step closer to building synthetic human DNA.

In May 2016, *Stat News* reported, he met with 130 scientists, lawyers, and government officials to discuss how development might proceed. Think about that for a moment. Church is not talking about editing the building blocks of human life. He wants to recreate them in a lab.

And it is more feasible and more far-reaching than most laypeople think.

To get there, the scientists will have to build on the pioneering work of Venter. In 2010, you'll recall, the geneticist led a team that created the first synthetic bacteria cell. What Church plans is much larger and more complex.

The potential reward is huge. Apart from giving scientists a better understanding of genetic code, it should provide insight into the complexity of gene relationships.

In "The Next Best Version of Me," an article appearing March 27, 2018, in *Wired*, David Ewing Duncan cites geneticist Charles Cantor, professor emeritus from Boston University. He thinks scientists are being too timid about what is possible.

"When I think of writing genomes," Cantor says, "I like to think of the different genres people could write. Personally, I like fiction—coming up with totally novel genomes, like making people who are engineered to get their energy from photosynthesis, or a plant that can walk."

And that is just the science. Yes, the idea of plants that can walk is weird.

The technology is getting better every day, too. Powerful public-cloud networks are more robust. Predictive data analytics and advanced modeling software are in a constant state of refinement. This will only improve as artificial intelligence comes into play. And the cost of compute continues to decline.

For investors, it's time to begin looking for ways to play this emergent technology.

> **HOW TO PLAY:** From analytical software, modeling and measurement, biotechnology, pharma, and medical devices, there are plenty of choices. A few include **Illumina** (ILMN), the leading maker of DNA sequencing machines; **Novartis** (NVS), a leading Swiss drug maker that has been an aggressive investor in immunotherapy; and **Abiomed** (ABMD), a pioneer in applying advanced statistical modeling to develop life-saving artificial heart valves.

Bioterrorism Could Kill 30 Million

Thirty million people dead in less than a year. That's the grisly forecast for a successful bioterrorist attack. And it's more likely than ever, according to experts.

Bill Gates made his fortune bringing personal computing to the world with Windows software. Lately he's been consumed with closing the window on the next global epidemic.

Advances in biotechnology mean it is now incredibly easy to recreate fast-moving, airborne pathogens, like smallpox or the Spanish flu.

Since the arrival of CRISPR-Cas9 gene editing in 2014, researchers have modified genes to help blind people see, cure sickle cell disease in some patients, and expedite the development of numerous new drug treatments.

They have also been able to create antibiotic-resistant forms of E. coli.

CRISPR-Cas9 is unregulated, inexpensive, and somewhat of a cottage industry. In 2016, the Nuffield Council of Bioethics warned that "garage scientists" might unwittingly create a modified organism that could kill millions.

Gates is thinking more strategically. His charitable foundation works in developing nations. He understands the perils of bad actors in unstable environments. He's worried about biotechnology being weaponized.

A single infected person strategically placed in a busy airport could ultimately kill millions.

"The scariest thing is something like the 1919 [Spanish] flu," Gates warned at a gathering at the Royal United Services Institute in London, in April 2017. Modern travel coupled with the fact that people have no immunity to that strain would be an unstoppable, deadly combination.

His concern is well founded. In the developed world, we worry about bad actors getting their hands on nuclear materials. Though tragic, a nuclear bomb would not kill 10 million people.

Gates reckons that an infected traveler could be the starting point for a human-to-human respiratory infection. And it would all begin with simple flu-like symptoms.

The Spanish Flu of 1919 killed up to 100 million people, around 5 percent of the world's population at the time.

While this is unsettling, we should not count out the good guys. The fact that Gates is involved is a big positive. He understands the scope of the potential problem, and he's making plans.

We also should not discount the potential for investors. Gene editing is a legitimate scientific breakthrough. Yet even to those who are well informed, it seems like science fiction. For the first time ever, scientists have a very precise tool to reprogram the genetic code of life. The possibilities are endless.

Researchers believe they can eradicate malaria by genetically modifying the mosquitos that carry the parasite. Malaria kills 1,000 children per day, and 200 million people are affected annually.

Others are working with innovative cancer-fighting immunology drugs and new HIV-AIDS treatments.

Drug discovery, treatment, and healthcare in general are at an inflection point. CRISPR-Cas9 has the potential to change everything by rewriting our genetic code.

> **HOW TO PLAY:** The threat of bioterrorism is real, but it's not the only possible outcome of genetic editing that matters. It's best for investors to focus on companies creating winners in the gene sequencing tools industry, led by **Illumina** (ILMN).

Better Crops Through Gene Editing

Scientists believe they can dramatically increase crop yields by tinkering with plant genomes.

Now investors finally have a pure play. In July 2017, **Calyxt Inc.** (CLXT) offered seven million shares, priced at $8, to the public to raise $56 million.

Although the tiny Minnesota concern bills itself as a consumer-centric food and agriculture company, the real investment story is gene editing.

Calyxt has a plan to use gene editing to change wheat.

It wants to fiddle with the bits of the genome that make certain types of wheat resistant to herbicides. Fixing that will increase crop yields. It is also working to increase fiber and produce new specialty ingredients, like healthier oils.

It might not seem like much, but it's an ambitious agenda with a potentially huge payoff.

Markets and Markets, an independent research firm, predicts the worldwide seed market will reach $113 billion by

2022. Monsanto accounts for a third of that. Its genetically modified organism seeds are especially dominant because they are so hearty.

Calyxt does not use GMOs. The strength of gene editing is that the genome is not being crossed with any foreign organism. Heartiness comes from editing away the weaker parts of the genome. In theory, that makes it safer.

A New Tool for Gene Editing

Homology Medicines (FIXX) built a better gene-editing platform. It came public in March 2018 and got off to a good start, rising to $21 from a starting price around $16, though it fell back to $17.50 within four months. It's hard for young companies to prove themselves quickly enough for Wall Street.

Gene editing sprang into the public consciousness with CRISPR-Cas9. Yet Homology has attracted attention by building what many in the industry believe to be a better editing tool.

Homology is focused on the single genetic mutations that cause rare, often fatal disorders. Based on the research of its founder, Dr. Saswati Chatterjee, a professor of virology at Beckman Research Institute, the company developed a proprietary gene-editing platform called AMEnDR.

What makes AMEnDR special is the discovery of adeno-associated virus vectors (AAVs) and the use of homologous recombination to correct gene mutations.

AAVs are naturally occurring, derived from human stem cells. After entering the bloodstream, they carry a corrected DNA element to the cell nucleus. That element targets and attaches itself to the mutated region in the genome. At that point, homologous recombination, a natural cellular process corrects the mutated gene.

The process has been found effective with both gene therapy and editing. Corrected DNA can be engineered to fix a single mutation or knock out and replace an entire gene. This opens up a potentially broad range of patients and multiple tissue uses, such as bone marrow, liver, lung, eye, and the central nervous system.

And the AAVs can be delivered intravenously in one setting.

This is cutting-edge science, and important. But is it still preclinical? All of the promise so far has been shown in laboratory mice.

Homology has set its drug development focus on very rare diseases, with no competing products. It is near phase 1 clinical trials for Adult Phenyleketonuria (PKU) and Pediatric PKU, an inherited disorder that results in increased proteins in the blood. Currently, PKU affects 50,000 people worldwide.

The company is also developing a gene transfer treatment for the central nervous system. It has gene correction projects targeting lung, liver, and human stem cells. In November 2017, it entered a collaboration for ophthalmic and sickle cell project development with Novartis, the giant Swiss pharmaceutical company.

The company raised $135 million in its IPO. Its shares are very risky, but may hold promise for patient investors who want to capitalize on this field and can accept the risk that it may never work out to investors' satisfaction.

Fast Forward

With just a few snips, developments that take nature centuries to accomplish scientists can do in hours with gene editing. The process is simply that of scientists who are using gene-editing tools to speed up evolution. It's removing the bad stuff to fix faulty genes. Jennifer Doudna, the cofounder of the CRISPR-Cas9 gene-editing technique, has said that the potential to dramatically increase food production is enormous. And, at least in theory, it is all perfectly safe because; unlike gene modification, there is no foreign material.

Lewis Ziska, a plant biologist at the US Department of Agriculture believes the process can be used to breathe nutrients into plant life that has been ravaged by pollution. Researchers are now editing animal DNA to produce proteins suitable for human medicines. Others, like George Church, want to build DNA by carefully manipulating molecules. All of this is exciting and potentially dangerous at the same time—and on the fast track.

It is also an opportunity for investors. I'm not one to invest in biotechnology stocks, as most of them fail. Making molecules is really hard. However, I am intrigued by Calyxt Inc. and Homology Medicines. These companies are potential home runs, though any company that swings for the fences is also prone to strike out.

To be sure, gene editing seems stranger than fiction. The thought that scientists are now capable of cutting away the bad parts of the genome almost seems too easy.

It's not easy. Not really. It has been a long, hard climb to this point. It is only possible because of better predictive analytics, larger stores of data to mine, and more powerful computer processing. It is a familiar theme in this fast-forward era. Technologies are converging, making breakthrough discoveries commonplace.

We are likely to see these discoveries first bear fruit in the production of healthier and more abundant food. Gene editing is a natural fit for agriculture because it amounts to simple subtraction. There is no addition of foreign materials, as with gene modification.

Other applications are coming, as scientists push new boundaries.

For investors, this should be an exciting time. Many smaller companies are going to make breakthroughs. However, caution is warranted. Most of these businesses will be single product and idea enterprises. Failure with that one effort will be catastrophic to shareholders.

HOW TO PLAY: Calyxt and Homology Medicines are interesting opportunities because managers are doing something different. The ideas are foundational, and if they pan out, the stocks will perform exceptionally well. For more stable stocks at the vanguard of the convergence of computing power and healthcare, stay focused on Illumina, Abiomed, and Novartis.

CHAPTER 12

PRECISION, NANO, AND REGENERATIVE MEDICINE: SCIENCE FICTION MEETS REALITY

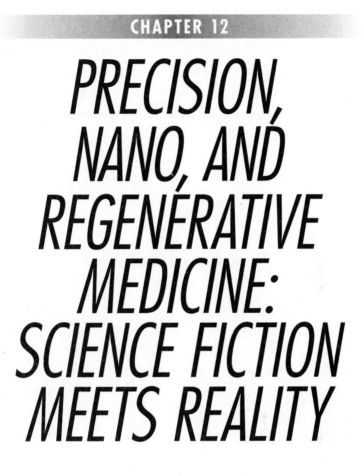

ata, predictive analytics, crazy fast supercomputers, and our understanding of the human genome have turned health sciences and drug discovery upside down. Traditional pharmaceutical companies are partnering with Silicon Valley stalwarts. Tech entrepreneurs are starting medical foundations. In May 2014, Samsung announced it wanted to start a drug business. Lines are being blurred. Medicine now looks more like computer science. That is a very good thing.

In this chapter I will show how this convergence is leading to real breakthroughs. I will drive into some of the wild projects—electric, and really small—that are in the pipeline. I will show how your smartphone may play a bigger role in future healthcare. I will also examine how a simple device might relieve the opioid crisis that is ravaging the country. And I will end with an unconventional stock pick, a consulting company working to fund many next-generation delivery strategies.

Personalized Medicine

One size shouldn't fit all.

Precision medicine promises to change health sciences by using data analytics and what we know about ourselves to tailor personal therapies and treatments.

Doctors should be able to use technology to deliver the right treatment to the right person at the right time. It all seems straightforward enough; getting to that point is more complex.

It started with the sequencing of the human genome. That project provided the road map to allow scientists to learn about illness at the cellular level, determine what precisely went wrong, and—at least in theory—determine a treatment for the mutation.

For example, most patients currently diagnosed with cancer undergo a battery of oncology tests and usually end up with surgery and chemotherapy. That one-size-fits-all treatment carpet bombs everything, killing good and bad cells indiscriminately.

Precision medicine is more of a smart bomb. Doctors locate the mutation at the cellular level, find the specific drug treatment to correct the abnormality, and calibrate the dosage based on personal metrics.

The theory is great. The only drawback is cost.

Technology is helping. Today, powerful cloud-based computers, using advanced algorithms, can sequence the human genome in less than a week for as little as a few thousand dollars. Soon it will be within the realm of possibility to screen every patient.

And it won't end with genes. Scientists are analyzing the microbes on our skin and in our gut. They are looking at environmental factors and even our diets to tailor treatments for illness that meet our individual needs. Sensor data from wearables like FitBit, smart watches, and smartphones will help, too.

True personalized medicine is coming.

In January 2015, President Obama announced that the administration would add $215 million to the annual budget for a comprehensive precision medicine plan. With bipartisan support—a rarity in the current political environment—the plan enlisted most of the leading medical facilitators.

The National Institutes of Health is helping to build a sample group of one million volunteers to draw more data. The National Cancer Institute will research the genomic drivers of cancer. The Food and Drug Administration will develop new testing techniques to expedite the drug approval process. And a consortium of privacy groups is being consulted to maintain strict privacy standards.

Pharmaceutical companies are gearing up. In 2015, Roche promised as much as $1 billion to **Blueprint Medicines** (BPMC) for five small molecule projects in development. Then, in January 2016, Roche announced it would spend another

$1 billion for a 56 percent stake in **Foundation Medicine**, a molecular and genomic diagnostic company. **Illumina** (ILMN), another diagnostic service provider, has formed similar alliances with Germany's Merck KGaA, AstraZeneca, and Sanofi.

Each of us is unique, a product of our own chemistry and environmental factors. It makes sense to build healthcare treatments tailored to that uniqueness. Ultimately it will be less costly and more effective. The evidence is piling up.

The key is getting more evidence. Precision medicine has the potential to create exciting new therapies and change the course of patient treatment. One of those personalized treatments, T-cell therapy, changed the life of a young leukemia patient named Emily. There will be many more success stories like her.

Patient Zero: Emily Whitehead

With a thick mop of wavy brown hair and a big toothy smile, Emily Whitehead looked like an average twelve-year-old.

Looks can be deceiving. She was the first child to receive CAR-T therapy, an innovative treatment that reengineers a patient's T-cells to fight aggressive cancers.

As a five-year-old, her parents, Tom and Kari, noticed she had become lethargic. Later, she began to develop bruises. Her gums would often bleed. After complaining of excruciating pain in her legs one evening, she was rushed to a hospital emergency room.

After several weeks of testing, her doctors concluded she was suffering from acute lymphoblastic leukemia, a treatable cancer with an 85 percent survival rate. However, Emily was an exception. After two intensive rounds of chemotherapy, the cancer continued to progress. Worse, she was not a suitable candidate for a bone marrow transplant.

As her condition worsened, Emily's parents reached out to the Children's Hospital of Philadelphia. Dr. Carl June, of the University of Pennsylvania, had been making exciting progress with mice and early stage human trials using an experimental treatment called CAR-T.

On April 17, 2012, Emily became his first pediatric patient.

First, doctors removed T-cells, often called the fighters of the immune system, from a blood sample. In the lab, these cells were multiplied and methodically reprogrammed to target and fight cancer. The fighter cells were then put back into Emily's body to target and kill cancer cells.

Side effects are normal. The purpose of the immune system is to fight outside infections. After Emily's third infusion, her temperature soared to 105 degrees. She had swelling in her extremities. Her blood pressure plummeted. She had trouble breathing as her lungs filled with fluid.

Her immune system had kicked into overdrive to reject the reengineered T-cells. Dr. June saw no recourse but to induce a medical coma, and cautioned Tom and Kari to expect the worse.

As a last-ditch effort, Dr. June prescribed a rheumatoid arthritis drug to relieve the inflammation. Although the treatment had never been used in that capacity, he hoped it might also suppress the immune response that put Emily in peril.

Fourteen days later, on her birthday, May 2, she woke up. Two weeks later, she was completely cancer free.

Today, she is a healthy girl. She likes Taylor Swift and sleepovers with her BFFs. She even got to meet her personal favorite, Lady Gaga. Emily and her family were special guests at the August 2017 launch of the Parker Institute for Cancer Immunotherapy in San Francisco.

She still goes to the hospital twice a month for B-cell replacement. Those cells were casualties of the CAR-T therapy. And she does suffer from Crohn's Disease. Otherwise, she is an average kid.

> **HOW TO PLAY:** The therapy is still a work in progress. A version developed by **Novartis** (NVS), the Swiss pharmaceutical giant, is in clinical tests around the world. Around half of the 175 pediatric patients that have received the treatment have entered full remission.

Former Napster Turns Immunotherapy Philanthropist

In April 2016, Sean Parker made headlines by donating $250 million to immune therapy cancer research.

Say and think what you will about the Silicon Valley billionaire, but Parker has shown an impeccable talent for attaching himself to winning ideas at just the right time.

In the summer of 1994, at age 15, Parker was into theoretical physics and hacking. Three years later, he and Shawn Fanning introduced peer-to-peer file sharing to the world with the music site Napster. A year later, that business had tens of millions of users.

In hacking circles, he was the closest thing to a rock star. That status helped him become the first president of Facebook in 2004.

Immunotherapy is where the Internet was in the early 2000s. It is certainly not new. For decades researchers, many of them Nobel Prize winning, have sought a way to harness the inherent prowess of the human immune system.

The concept is simple: The immune system has powerful agents called T-cells that seek out and destroy harmful invading viruses and infection, so why not use these same weapons to fight cancer? It makes perfect sense except it was quickly discovered that cancer and other maladies like human immunodeficiency virus (HIV) are often able to hide from T-cells.

In 1992, Japanese scientists determined the reason for this evasion was a special molecule on T-cells, which they labeled "program death 1" (PD1). Disrupting PD1 has met with varying degrees of success. In some cases, new drugs were temporarily effective. In other cases, the results were catastrophic, with T-cells destroying cells indiscriminately and causing patient death.

Enter gene editing and big data. By snipping and fixing DNA, researchers have been able to modify T-cells to make them more effective cancer warriors.

The biotechnology firm Cellectis used the TALENs gene-editing process to construct T-cells that specifically found and destroyed blood cell abnormalities common to leukemia. In the first celebrated case, this procedure led to the complete cure of a British toddler. Since then 300 additional patients have enjoyed mostly spectacular results.

In 2015, Alphabet—the parent of Google—held a conference with leading oncologists and biologists at Massachusetts Institute of Technology expressly to determine what parts of the process could benefit from its expertise in machine learning and compute power.

Its biotechnology subsidiary, Verily, is now believed to be

working on therapies that evolve from better understanding of how T-cells attack cancer within the tumor.

Jeffrey Hammerbacker, the former Facebook big data guru, is now at Mount Sinai Hospital in New York. There, he and 12 programmers are developing software that determines how a person's DNA can be optimized to build better cancer-fighting T-cells. By most accounts, the science is still about two years away from legitimate curative medicines. However, the discovery process is accelerating as information technology progresses.

And this would be an extraordinary discovery.

Two of the leading immunotherapy enterprises, **Kite Pharmaceuticals** and **Juno Therapeutics**, were swallowed by Gilead Sciences in August 2017, and Celgene Corp. in January 2018, respectively.

Big pharma is circling. Good things are near.

Sean Parker put himself in the middle of genetically modified immune cell therapies. In 2016, the Parker Institute for Cancer Immunotherapy launched with 40 laboratories, 300 researchers, and six of the leading cancer centers in the United States.

New York's Memorial Sloan Kettering; Stanford Medicine; the University of California, Los Angeles; the University of California, San Francisco; Houston's University of Texas MD Anderson; and the University of Pennsylvania in Philadelphia were founding partners.

By March 2018, the ranks of leading cancer centers had swollen to ten. Boston's Dana-Farber Cancer Institute, Fred Hutchinson Cancer Research Center in Seattle, Icahn School of Medicine at Mount Sinai of New York, and the Washington School of Medicine in St. Louis are all exchanging data.

Parker told Axios in March 2018 that the number of affiliated labs now exceeds 60. The number of industry and non-profit partners has grown to 40.

And best of all, the labs, researchers, and cancer centers will share data. It is a throwback to his Napster days. The institute is a peer-to-peer network. By exchanging data quickly and transparently, everyone on the network gets the most complete version of the truth.

The idea is to disrupt the conventional discovery process.

Initially, researchers will focus on modifying personal T-cells, boosting patient responses to immunotherapy drugs, and developing innovative ways to attack cancer tumors.

These therapies hold potential cures for autoimmune disorders including multiple sclerosis, lupus, HIV, arthritis, diabetes, and the big one, cancer. That's not bad for a guy who started out building software to help teens steal music online.

HOW TO PLAY: In 2018, there are few ways to invest directly in immunotherapy. Investors looking for some exposure should look to larger pharmaceutical firms like Gilead Sciences (GILD), Johnson & Johnson (JNJ), and Amgen (AMGN).

Google Electrifies Medical Research

In August 2016, GlaxoSmithKline and Verily Life Sciences made a startling announcement. Together, they believe they can bring tiny implantable robots to medicine.

The pharmaceutical industry has made tremendous gains in medicine. Until now, all have been achieved through better chemistry. It is the basis of modern medicine. Glaxo and Verily believe there is another way. Clinicians have made significant medical progress by regulating, and in some cases changing, electrical impulses to the nervous system.

The goal is to take that research to the next level with implanted machines no bigger than a grain of rice. They'll attach themselves to tissue in our lungs, gut, and other regions. They will zap nerves and hopefully change the way our bodies deal with chronic illnesses like asthma, Crohn's Disease, diabetes, and even arthritis.

If all of this sounds a lot like the plot of 1966 film *Fantastic Voyage*, that's because it is—minus the cheesy special effects and Raquel Welch in a jumpsuit. But the science is strong.

In October 2015, the research division at the Pentagon announced a project based on similar science.

The Defense Advanced Research Projects Agency selected seven leading research facilities. The goal of the $80 million project, called ElectRx, was to map the neural circuitry of the human body and determine how sensors and motor signals affect changes in the human brain and organs.

In the DARPA announcement press release, Doug Weber, the project manager, said ElectRx supposes there is a system of protocols that moderates functions in the brain, spinal cord, and internal organs to maintain health. Finding and learning how to stimulate those protocols should be the key to health.

It is a simple theory with plenty of basis in data. The most direct evidence is the modern pacemaker. A simple electronic device uses pulses of regulated electricity to stimulate and force the heart to beat at a healthy rate.

ElectRx is a pacemaker for the peripheral nervous system, Weber explains.

Initially, DARPA has been focused on inflammatory diseases like rheumatoid arthritis and chronic pain. There is a simple reason. Researchers believe post-traumatic stress disorder, a disease rampant among returning soldiers, is the product of excess levels of biomolecules in the body.

In theory, finding a way to regulate those levels would be a minimally invasive way to bring comfort to many thousands of veterans.

Through mid-2018, the project involves seven development teams with a robust software and medical device pedigree. Researchers at Circuit Therapeutics of Menlo Park, New York's Columbia University, the Florey Institute of Neuroscience in Australia, John's Hopkins University in Baltimore, MIT in Cambridge, Purdue University in Indiana, and the University of Texas in Dallas will divvy up $80 million in funding.

The GSK/Verily partnership is even bigger.

The companies invested a total of $715 million in August 2016 in a brand new bioelectronics business they call Galvani Bioelectronics. The new unit set up research facilities near its parents' digs north of London, and in San Francisco. There, the teams totaling 30 scientists and clinicians pool existing intellectual property and have begun the process of studying and building tiny battery powered devices.

GSK and Verily bring very different skill sets to the new 55/45 joint venture. The British pharmaceutical giant adds its long history of biology, drug development, and delivery. Verily brings its expertise in software architecture, data analytics, electrical engineering, and miniaturization.

The new company takes its name from Luigi Galvani, the Italian researcher who is considered the father of neuroscience. He gained fame by animating severed frog legs with a type of static electricity in 1780.

While that might seem like a strange way to spend time

in the eighteenth century, keep in mind doctors continue to use the precepts of that seminal work today with pacemakers. Galvani Bioelectronics plans to follow that lead too, only with substantially smaller gear.

This has been a focus of GSK for some time. Since 2012 it's been pouring money into the nascent field with zeal. Moncef Slaoui, the chairman of its global vaccines unit, explained: "This agreement with Verily to establish Galvani Bioelectronics signals a crucial step forward in GSK's bioelectronics journey, bringing together health and tech to realize a shared vision of miniaturized, precision electrical therapies. Together, we can rapidly accelerate the pace of progress in this exciting field, to develop innovative medicines that truly speak the electrical language of the body."

It's hard to imagine that technology has reached the point where scientists are serious about tiny implanted robots capable of fighting chronic illness. Yet, some of the brightest minds in pharmaceutical research and data science believe it is both possible and transformational.

Galvani Bioelectronics is not yet a public company, and Verily represents a tiny part of Alphabet.

We Need to Think Even Smaller

You know who saw all of this coming long ago? Ray Kurzweil.

In January 2016, standing before a conference audience in Vancouver, he told attendees that in 25 years, computers would be one billion times more powerful per dollar and 100,000 times smaller.

He was speaking of a field called nanotechnology. It takes

its name from *nanometer*, a measurement. One nanometer is 1/1,000,000,000th of a meter, or 1/100th the width of a human hair.

We are not talking about implantable computers the size of a grain of rice. Kurzweil is predicting that computers will be the size of blood cells. Imagine what would be possible.

Before you dismiss all of this as quackery, you should know previous Kurzweil predictions have been uncanny. In his 1990 book, *The Age of Intelligent Machines*, he predicted the Internet would become the defining consumer technology of our generation.

Considering CompuServe and Prodigy together accounted for little more than one million users at the time, it seemed like crazy talk.

And then there were his predictions about the rise of mobile phones, fax machines, and even the fall of the Soviet Union. In later books he said we should expect supercomputers in the cloud and wireless, wearable computing devices. At the time, all of these ideas seemed outside the realm of possibility.

Yet today, powerful cloud-computing networks power our cities, communications, and the smartphones we cannot seem to live without. The latest Apple Watch can independently monitor the wearer's heart rate and blood oxygen level.

And Kurzweil, by all accounts, is a genius. He is a very successful inventor. By rethinking the way light is sent, collected, and delivered by sensors, he created the first CCD flatbed scanner. It is a technology we now take for granted in modern home printers. He invented the first print-to-speech reading machine for the blind. He invented the modern synthesizer.

Those Kurzweil keyboards you see at concerts and music videos—that's him.

In 1999, he received the National Medal of Technology and Innovation. In 2002 he was inducted into the National Inventors Hall of Fame. *Inc.* magazine called him "Edison's rightful heir." He has been a professor at MIT. And since 2012, he's been the head engineer at Google.

When computers are so small they can be easily delivered into the blood stream, he says, humans will cure most diseases. They will diagnose illnesses and dispatch tiny computers with the appropriate drug treatments.

Kurzweil predicts most of this will occur in the 2030s. In the interim, researchers are working with the tools they have to deliver targeted drug treatments or blast away cancer cells.

Most of the excitement has centered on nanoparticles.

The first FDA-approved nanoparticle treatment occurred in 1995 when Doxil was approved. The treatment was used for adult cancers such as ovarian, multiple myeloma, and Karposi sarcoma, a rare form of cancer associated with HIV/AIDS.

The attraction of nanoparticles is drug treatment delivery. Because the particles can be engineered, they can get to places traditional treatments cannot. Very often, they are designed to bind to cancer cells and deliver the drug treatment to a specific location. This is very different than most treatments that impact general locations.

Researchers at Durham University in the United Kingdom, and Rice University in the United States, are making real progress.

In September 2016, the research teams jointly published a paper in *Nature*, the respected science journal. The researchers have been able to build tiny molecular machines governed by light that are capable of killing cancer cells.

It's the beginning of noninvasive surgery. And it's going to be a huge investment opportunity.

Scientists have been trying to mobilize molecular structures for a long time. They strung together molecules in the shape of cars and submarines. The goal was to develop nanomachines capable of creating enough momentum to push through the natural currents in the human body, and eventually penetrate cells.

James Tour, professor of Chemistry, Computer Science, Material Science, and Nanotechnology at Rice, believes there has been a breakthrough.

His team increased the effectiveness of the nanomachines by including addends. These additional molecules have specific functions, like recognizing and attaching to targeted cells. For example, peptide addends are used to recognize human prostate cancer cells. The nanomachine moves through the body, looking for those cells. When they are located, the machines attach to the cancer cells.

They are dormant until they are activated by ultraviolet light. Then the powerful rotors begin spinning.

Tour and the team at Durham have been able to build molecular machines that spin at a rate of two to three million revolutions per second. That's fast enough to burrow through cell walls.

In animal tests, the machines have been able to annihilate cancers and other tumors in seconds.

They are powerful, tiny, and utilitarian. Tour says around 50,000 nanomachines can fit across the diameter of a human hair. And in the near future he expects they will be able to carry pharmaceuticals. They will seek the targeted cancer cells, burrow holes, and then place the necessary drug treatment.

There is another key component. According to reporting from *The Telegraph*, the machines are completely harmless until they are activated by ultraviolet light. This means they are perfect for treatment of breast tumors, skin melanomas, and cancers that are especially resistant to chemotherapy.

"It's going to be a whole new way to treat patients," Tour said in a YouTube video promoting the research.

In September 2017, researchers at Caltech built nanoscale DNA robots capable of picking up other DNA material. While these are not the miniature computers promised by Kurzweil, they are tiny mechanical structures.

In February 2018, teams of scientists from Arizona State University and the National Center for Nanoscience and Technology of the Chinese Academy of Sciences published new findings in *Nature*. They have had success stopping and, in some cases, killing cancer tumors by injecting mice and pigs with nanobots constructed from sheets of DNA.

Measuring 60–90 nanometers, these sheets of DNA are folded like origami. The outside of the structure consists of a protein that is present in the lining of blood vessels associated with tumors. The inside carries a package of thrombin molecules, an agent that causes blood to clot.

When the nanorobot reaches its target, molecules called aptamers force the folds open, releasing the blood clotting thrombin. The nanorobot effectively starves the tumor of the oxygen it needs to grow by choking off the blood supply. It is a simple, effective strategy borrowed from angiogenesis inhibitors, a category of cancer-fighting treatments that kill by strangulation.

What makes origami nanorobots different is the precision. Their molecular composition naturally draws them to the tumor. And because the molecules can be engineered, the bots are very maneuverable.

The other attraction is biology. DNA nanorobots are less likely to be rejected easily by the immune system.

It is still early, and these are really big ideas. But they are out there, and increasing computer power and better information technology makes discovery more likely.

In the interim, life sciences companies are picking the low-hanging fruit. They are repacking the technology we already have to cut costs and save lives.

HOW TO PLAY: Pfizer (PFE), the American pharmaceutical giant, has been working closely with a number of start-ups, including 23andMe, a DNA data collection firm backed by both Google Ventures and Genentech, and **Johnson and Johnson** (JNJ).

Patients, Your Smartphone Will See You Now

Providing healthcare is a giant pain. Escalating costs and an aging population are causing a political divide. They are also pushing government budgets to the breaking point.

Two start-ups have a fix. Doctor on Demand and Healthy. io want to use software and the smartphones most of us can't live without to slash costs and revolutionize healthcare.

As the name suggests, Doctor on Demand focuses on scheduling. The software facilitates video consultations using a smartphone. After the session, the doctor can order tests or even write prescriptions.

Think of it as face time, but with your doctor.

For Hill Ferguson, chief executive of the San Francisco start-up, the big benefit is empowerment. The patient gets to decide when the consultation happens and even where the lab work is completed. That is a big improvement over being "told where to go by your provider," says Ferguson.

Healthy.io is pushing the smartphone angle even further. It wants to turn the device into a piece of medical equipment. The process starts with a physical test kit sent by mail. Users provide a urine sample on a card, scan the results with their smartphone camera, and send that data to the doctor. The analysis happens immediately.

Cutting out the laboratory opens up more efficient opportunities for early detection. In the long run, these factors slash the cost of providing care.

According to reports from the Centers for Medicare and Medicaid Services, the United States spent $3.2 trillion on healthcare in 2015, or $9,990 per person. And the national health expenditure grew 5.8 percent in 2015, representing 17.8 percent of the gross domestic product.

This means the United States spends more for healthcare than any other country. While it makes sense—rich countries spend more on services, it is not clear that the United States is deriving appropriate value.

Many studies show that America does not receive superior outcomes despite high expenditures. In fact, health outcomes continually fall below the United Kingdom, another rich country, despite spending roughly three times more per capita.

Technology companies hope software can change that. In April 2017, Verily, the Alphabet subsidiary, announced a 10,000-person, four-year study in conjunction with Stanford and Duke universities.

Each subject will wear a custom wrist sensor capable of continuously collecting heart data. Additionally, every year, they will undergo detailed medical tests, offering blood, sweat, urine, and even tears. The goal is to digitalize everything and then use powerful machine-learning software to learn more about general health and preventative measures to reduce costs.

The past two decades have seen a software revolution spawned by digitalization. Software changed the way we consume media and buy products and services. Decidedly, analog experiences were transformed into bits of data that could be manipulated and optimized with software. The result was plummeting costs.

HOW TO PLAY: The best way to play this trend is **Apple** (AAPL). The iPhone maker has been very active in healthcare, as it parlays its large installed base into a services empire.

New Device Eases Agony of Kicking Opioids

The opioid epidemic ravages small and large towns across America.

And it has largely been intractable both to law enforcement and to the medical community. Until now.

In November 2017, the Food and Drug Administration approved the first electronic device for the treatment of opioid withdrawal. For the government, it is an all-hands-on-deck moment.

The device, Neuro-Stim System-2 Bridge, looks like a large

hearing aid with four wires. Doctors can affix the device behind a patient's ear. Then they attach its stimulation electrodes to nerve centers near and in the ear.

When the patient feels pain, the device intercedes. It sends low-frequency electric impulses to the part of the brain that receives and processes pain signals.

Within moments, patients feel pain free.

The idea behind NSS-2 is not new. Neuromodulators have been around since the mid-1960s.

Researchers found they could block pain by stimulating parts of the nervous system with electric impulses. Think of the process as a form of electronic acupuncture.

The NSS-2 innovation is delivery. A trained professional can adhere the device in minutes. It requires no surgery or narcotics. Symptoms are relieved almost immediately, allowing the patient to resume normal activities without restrictions.

And at an average cost of $600 per unit, it is cost effective.

That is a small price to pay to move people from addiction. According to a 2016 report from the American Society of Addiction Medicine, two million Americans were addicted to opioid painkillers, and 591,000 were addicted to heroin. During 2015, drug overdose was the leading cause of accidental death in the United States.

Newsweek recently reported that researchers at the University of Illinois estimate heroin use costs US taxpayers $51 billion annually. Spiraling costs for incarceration, healthcare, and lost productivity are widespread in afflicted communities. In Smalltown USA, these problems are catastrophic.

Ross County is a rural community of 77,000, one hour south of Columbus, Ohio. The county placed 200 children into state care in 2016. A shocking 75 percent of those children came from families with parents who were wrestling with opioid addiction. And caring for these children is more expensive because they require special counseling and therapy as well as longer stays.

For a tiny community, the $2.4 million price tag is a budget buster.

While NSS-2 will not wipe out the crisis, it will help. Opioid withdrawal is painful. Common symptoms include muscle aches and pains, vomiting, diarrhea, and uncontrollable shaking. Many addicts continue to use the drug because they deem it impossible to get through the withdrawal process.

The FDA has approved NSS-2 for opioid addiction treatment. And the Trump Administration has declared a national opioid crisis.

All this means more taxpayer money is coming into the system. It means more treatment, better quality of life for addicts, and healthier finances for ravaged communities.

The opportunity for investors may not be immediately obvious. Innovative Health Solutions, the company behind NSS-2, is a private company based in Versailles, Indiana.

However, several of the businesses likely to administer the devices and care for the patients are public companies. These are relatively small enterprises. The opportunity at hand will have a material impact on cash flow and profitability. It should also favorably impact shareholder value.

Down the value chain, expect insurers like Cigna and Aetna to be favorably impacted as well.

The opioid crisis is a blight on our culture. Thankfully, some help is on the way.

More direct but much riskier stock plays include **Express Scripts** (ESRX), a pharmacy benefits manager; **AAC Holdings**

Inc. (AAC), a substance abuse treatment center operator; and **Opiant Pharmaceuticals Inc.** (OPNT), a developer of substance abuse pharmacological treatments.

Accenture Designs the New Healthcare Business Plan

Like most great businesses, Accenture was born out of competition.

Long before it got a fancy name, the company was Anderson Consulting, the business and consulting wing of the global professional services firm Anderson Worldwide Societe Cooperative, or AWSC.

AWSC was a fiercely competitive environment. Managers pitted divisions against each other to wring out inefficiencies and spur innovation.

For years Anderson Consulting went head-to-head with its sister company, Arthur Anderson, a global accounting firm. Under the AWSC charter, the more profitable business was to receive a bonus of 15 percent of the profits of the sister company.

But Arthur Anderson had a distinct advantage. It was a larger business with broader reach. And in 1998, managers at the accounting firm pushed the envelope by launching an internal business consulting division. Suddenly, two divisions inside AWSC were competing for the same clients.

Something had to give.

Anderson Consulting managers decided to stop paying the 15 percent penalty. They claimed both AWSC and Arthur Anderson had breached the contract. They took the entire matter to the International Chamber of Commerce.

In 2000, an arbitration agreement ensued. Anderson Consulting paid $1.2 billion and agreed to change its name. In 2001, Accenture, short for accent on the future, was born. Five months later, it became a public company, listed on the New York Stock Exchange.

The history of Accenture is important. Executives have always been forced to manage smaller than the company footprint. They have religiously cut costs to enhance profitability. It is in the corporate DNA.

In 2018, Accenture had 425,000 mostly professional employees. They service clients in 200 countries. In 2015, the company employed 130,000 people in India. Fifty thousand more were domiciled in the Philippines. It is not an accident. Professionals there are plentiful. Wages and rents are low relative to more developed countries.

In 2017, Accenture had gross income of $11.15 billion on sales of $36.77 billion. That puts gross margins at 30 percent.

Other financial metrics are equally impressive. Accenture has been able to achieve an average of 18.7 percent return on assets during the past five years. Over the same time frame, the return on equity is 56.4 percent. The return on invested capital is 55.9 percent.

And the very best part of the story is the future is even brighter.

The entire corporate world is beginning a digital transformation. Processes that used to be analog are becoming digital.

Accenture is running professional services on behalf of governments. In 2014, Accenture won a $563 million contract for software development and ongoing professional services for Healthcare.gov. In 2015 it was part of the winning group for a $4.33 billion contract for electronic health records, awarded by the Department of Defense.

These contracts are about digital transformation.

Accenture has other healthcare irons in the fire. It's a big player in Population Health, or Care Management, that involves delivering cost-saving recommendations to a single payer, like the government, a corporate enterprise, or a health insurance provider.

If Accenture can deliver, it wins a share of the cost savings.

The idea is develop winning protocols. Accenture would use its long history of cost cutting to help with early detection, preventative measures, or strategies to reduce expensive emergency room visits.

According to Grandview Research, the size of the population health research—aimed at preventive care and promoting well-being—is expected to reach $89.5 billion by 2025. For perspective, in 2015, the market was worth $20.7 billion.

It is a market ripe for disruption. It's a market Accenture is poised to win.

Winning is what Accenture does best. It is taking its digital transformation message to governments and corporations with stunning results.

According to the company fact sheet, Accenture claims 95 of the Fortune Global 100, and 75 percent of the Fortune Global 500. In other words, when big corporations turn to managing consultants, it is most likely Accenture.

Very often the company is running mission-critical operations on behalf of the client. And its reach spans every sector.

Financial results in the past few years have been rock solid, regularly beating analyst estimates, as growth accelerated across every part of the business.

Its work with financial services, communications, media, and technology firms is on the rise as more companies embrace digital.

The company is a winner, and managers are determined to create shareholder value by helping other large entities find their way thoughtfully and aggressively in the digital age. In addition to reporting strong results quarter after quarter, the company is an aggressive buyer of its common stock. It's a buy on pullbacks.

Fast Forward

When it comes to health sciences in discussions about technological progress, health sciences are often overlooked. Approval processes take too long. There is too much red tape and too many intermediaries.

It's true. Healthcare has not been disrupted at all since 2000. However, a digital transformation is coming, and data changes everything. Some of the same people that disrupted computer networking, ecommerce, and media have turned their focus to medicine. They understand what is possible with unprecedented amounts of data, analytics, and fast computer processing.

And it is hard to argue with the success stories in immunotherapy or the promise of nanotechnology. Everything is finally falling into place for better and more efficient therapies—and outcomes.

INDEX